STRAIGHT TO THE MONEY

STRAIGHT TO THE MONEY

The Definitive Guide to Changing Your Mindset, Outlook, and Behaviors to Attract Wealth

ROSE M. BELLEFLEUR

PLUTUS PUBLISHING
ATLANTA, GA

STRAIGHT TO THE MONEY:
THE DEFINITIVE GUIDE TO CHANGING YOUR MINDSET, OUTLOOK, AND BEHAVIORS TO ATTRACT WEALTH

The information provided within this book is for general informational and educational purposes only. The author does not guarantee results and makes no representations or warranties, express or implied, about the completeness, accuracy, reliability, suitability or availability with respect to the information, products, services, or related graphics contained in this book for any purpose. Any use of this information is at your own risk.

Paperback ISBN-13: 978-0-578-77786-3

Published by Plutus Publishing
Atlanta, GA

Printed in the United States of America
First Edition Feburary 2021

Cover and Interior Design by: Make Your Mark Publishing Solutions
Editing by: Make Your Mark Publishing Solutions

This book is dedicated to my late grandmother, Emma Rose Bellefleur.

Contents

Introduction

So, I may have lied, specifically regarding this book's title. Truth be told, *Straight to the Money: Get off Your Ass and Do the Damn Work* isn't as catchy, friendly, or enticing a title as *Straight to the Money: The Definitive Guide to Changing Your Mindset, Outlook, and Behaviors to Attract Wealth* (not to mention, my mom and dad would be mortified if I used the words "ass" and "damn" in the title of my book). You see, contrary to the millennial, self-help bullshit floating around, you can't simply *attract* wealth. If that were the case, with a few attitude tweaks, we'd all be guaranteed millionaires. When it comes to wealth, unless you are being fed from a silver spoon, you must do the work. But it's hard to do the work when you haven't got the faintest clue of where or even how to get started. That's where this book comes in, to educate you on the eight fundamental rules of building wealth.

This book will require three things from you. First, read the book in its entirety. Second, read it more than once, and third, implement the principles discussed in this book into your everyday life.

For someone who is riddled with credit card debt, implementing the concepts behind this book into your everyday life may look like putting one of your credit card bills on autopay and making minimum payments instead of completely ignoring the bill until it goes to collections. For someone who feels as if homeownership is out of their reach, this may look like attending a free first-time homebuyer's course hosted by your local real estate agent. The "how" and "why" behind everyone's implementation will be different, but I need you to go into this book with the knowledge that when you're done reading it, you'll need to step outside of your comfort zone and commit to making, at minimum, one change in your financial behaviors.

Now that I've gotten that confession off my chest and set some expectations, we can get started.

RULE #1

Transform Your Mindset to One Geared Toward Wealth

You can read all the wealth books in the world, sign up for every financial literacy workshop, and repost as many #wealth, #debtfreecommunity, and #financialfreedom posts you want, but if you have a poverty mindset, all these actions will be in vain. Now, you're probably wondering, *What is a poverty mindset?* It's a mindset based on damaging perceptions, negative self-talk, constant complaining, and the inability to accept responsibility for your actions.

How Do You Perceive the World?

The thing about perception is that it drives your behavior and alters your actions, moods, and emotions, turning false negative thoughts into the truth, a self-fulfilling prophecy to be exact. For many, their perception is so shrouded in negativity that it has them living a dreadful reality.

We've all been there. Maybe it's cloudy and dreary outside, or you've awakened on the wrong side of the bed, but in one moment, the fate of your entire day is decided. You're convinced you are going to have a bad day. You hit the snooze button and stay in bed a while longer. It would be one thing if you took those few extra minutes to relax, but you don't. Instead, you're in bed, brooding and anxiously dreading the day ahead of you. You rise out of bed, your feet hit the ground, and the wrath of destruction brought on by your negative perception begins. You half-ass your morning routine, which causes you to leave your badge, wallet, and lunch at home. You hit the worst part of morning traffic, which guarantees you're going to be late.

At this point, you could put an end to this terrible day. You could calmly sit in traffic, send your team a quick note warning them you're going to be fifteen minutes late, and make peace with the rough start you've had, but you don't. Instead, you swerve in and out of lanes, cut other drivers off, and spend your morning commute honking and making R-rated gestures to others. You arrive at work late and go through an entire debacle with security because you don't have your badge. Your morning is harried as you go through the motions of this terrible day, snapping at coworkers and doing your work with what little energy and enthusiasm you can spare. Your breaking point comes during lunch when you realize you've left your food and wallet at home. *The devil is busy,* you tell yourself, when in fact, it's you who has been busy, thought by thought and action by action, bringing a terrible day to fruition.

The moral of the story? Someone who wakes up thinking their day is going to go horribly will subconsciously change their actions, little by little, in a negative manner until this prediction becomes true. You've probably noticed a pattern; when you repeatedly look at your situation through a negative lens, the negativity always comes to life. If you are constantly dwelling on "how broke you are," you'll notice you seem to perpetually remain broke. If you are always dwelling on how hard life has been for you compared to your friends, you'll notice your path is always a bit more daunting than theirs.

A negative perception is an aspect of a poverty mindset. With a negative perception, you perceive people, situations, and things in a negative light and subconsciously work to make these perceptions your truth. When this negative outlook comes to fruition, you act like the Universe has conspired against you while failing to acknowledge the role you've played with your behavior.

Is Your Internal Dialogue Negative or Positive?

In addition to damaging perceptions, negative self-talk is also a component of a poverty mindset. Self-talk is the internal dialogue you experience daily as you go through situations and process information, emotions, or events. It is the voice in your head. Self-talk is a culmination of your conscious thoughts, as well as your unconscious assumptions, biases, and beliefs.[1]

"I need to practice before I make that presentation," "It might be challenging, but I've got the skills and experience to conquer this," or "I'm going to crush my workout at the gym today" are examples of reasonable or positive self-talk. Self-talk is incredibly useful when it's positive, as it helps one overcome fears and bolsters confidence. However, when self-talk is negative, it can be crippling. "I don't have the resources to do this," "I can't do anything right," or "I don't have much of a future" are a few examples of negative self-talk. Negative self-talk tends to be unrealistic and harmful, and can paralyze the thinker into inaction, rumination, and self-absorption.

What's worse is the average person will confidently tell you they don't engage in negative self-talk, but below are examples of negative self-talk surrounding finances and wealth many people think to themselves regularly:

- I'm too old to go after my dreams.
- I am poor.
- I am so broke.
- I'm an idiot when it comes to my finances.
- I'm terrible at managing my money.
- Everyone else is doing so much better than me.
- I'll never pay off my credit card debt.
- Money goes out for me faster than it comes in.

These statements might seem like just words to some, but after repeating and dwelling on them for years, you begin to believe them and subconsciously align your actions to these statements.

Negative self-talk is associated with high levels of stress and low self-esteem, both of which are correlated to a lack of motivation and feelings of helplessness. Trust me; you don't need a lack of motivation and feelings of helplessness on your journey to financial freedom and wealth.

Those who engage in negative self-talk live in a reality where they can't reach the goals they've set for themselves. They have a lowered ability to see opportunities around them and, therefore, cannot capitalize on them.

Besides stress and lower self-esteem, negative self-talk has additional consequences on one's life and mental health:[2]

- You've told yourself so often that you can't do certain things, you begin to believe it.
- You strive for perfection, which isn't realistic. This need for perfection leads you to think your "great" and "good" aren't enough.

Other Signs of Having a Poverty Mindset

I know what you're thinking: "There are more signs of having a poverty mindset?" The unfortunate answer is yes. I understand you might be feeling attacked or even triggered at this point, but stay with me a little while longer because there are two additional aspects of a poverty mindset that I need to educate you on: always playing the blame game and constantly complaining.

Always Playing the Blame Game

A telltale sign of having a poverty mindset is always playing the blame game. Those with a poverty mindset blame everyone but themselves. It's the government's fault, their parents' fault, their spouse's fault, or their boss's fault. The common theme: It's never their fault. The problem always lies with someone or something else. But truthfully, it isn't anything or anyone else.

There's a problem many fail to see when playing the blame game. Blaming others allows you to create excuses for why you cannot or have not succeeded. This mentality is disempowering, as it shifts the blame to everyone else and doesn't allow you to take full accountability for your life.

Constantly Complaining

Another sign of having a poverty mindset is continuously complaining. When you complain, you are dwelling on the negative. When people complain, they never talk about the good; they focus on the bad.

When was the last time someone gave you an earful on how *amazing* their life is going? I'm sure it's been a while. People typically go on and on about how stressful, frustrating, and crazy their week has been by recounting the "craziest thing" that happened to them since the last time you spoke to them. What's worse, complaining like this can become a habit. When you've spent so much time focusing on the bad, it's hard to look at things in a positive light. People who complain all the time become masters at finding the bad in situations, no matter the good.

Those who love complaining find no greater delight than being in the presence of other complainers. Together, they swap war stories about their annoying spouses, ill-behaved children, horrific bosses, or whatever horrendous plight they believe they are facing. Never is the energy and time dedicated to complaining redirected toward positivity or an escape route. Instead, it becomes a game, with the reward going to who can complain the loudest.

Going from a Poverty Mindset to One That Attracts Wealth

The good news is with a few tweaks and lifestyle changes, you can easily transition to a mindset geared toward wealth, despite spending most of your life with a poverty mindset fueled by negative thoughts, negative perceptions, constant complaining, and playing the blame game. How do you go about making this transition? By rewiring your brain with positive affirmations targeted toward your finances to manifest positivity, wealth, and abundance into your life.

Affirmations are statements that are recited to encourage and motivate the person speaking them. These powerful mantras induce a positive mindset, as they root to your subconscious and conscious mind to influence your actions and habits. They result in the affirmer seeing things differently and viewing themselves in a newer, more positive light. This positive viewpoint will inspire you to start making exciting changes and finding solutions rather than focusing on problems.

What's the Purpose of Affirmations?

Affirmations do two things. First, they allow you to become aware of your subconscious negative thoughts by bringing them to the surface. And second, they enable you to bring your goals, whether short-term or long-term, to the forefront of your mind. A few powerful money affirmations you may want to keep in your arsenal include:

- I am deserving of abundance and wealth in my life.
- My cup runs over.
- Money steadily flows to me.
- The more I give, the more I receive. The more I receive, the more I give.
- I am worthy of a prosperous life.
- My success is imminent.

Creating Your Positive Affirmations

You can even create your own positive affirmations using the following steps:

1. Think of some negative thoughts you hold regarding your finances.
2. Instead of bottling these thoughts in, write your most pressing thoughts on a sheet of paper.
3. On the other side of the paper, write the opposite of these negative thoughts. These will be the positive affirmations that are going to replace the negative thoughts.
    - When doing this part of the exercise, start with the phrases "I am," "I know," or "I have" versus "I want" or "I need," as you don't want to affirm the feeling of wanting and needing.

    - Keep the affirmations short and to the point.

    - Write your affirmations in the present tense and avoid putting a time frame on them.

    - Keep the affirmation realistic. An affirmation, like "I am going to be a millionaire," for someone who is unemployed and on the verge of eviction is most likely not going to be effective. This affirmation is too far from reality to be accepted by your subconscious mind. A better assertion for someone in this financial state would be "I am improving my finances every day" or "I am finding resources and opportunities to earn money." As you say these affirmations in tandem with setting and conquering small financial goals, you can then begin to affirm "I am going to be a millionaire." At this point, your subconscious mind would not reject this affirmation.

- When saying your affirmations, think of the positive feelings associated with them. You want to feel what you are manifesting. Imagine how amazing it's going to feel when you send in your final student loan payment, make your last payment toward your credit card debt, or reach your savings goal. Every time you say your affirmations, you want to conjure these positive and joyful emotions.

- Keep the affirmation entirely positive. Instead of affirming "I am not broke," you would simply say, "I am rich." Although it's tempting to use the word "broke" in a positive context, it is still a negative word associated with negative emotions. Despite affirming "I am not broke," you will feel the feelings associated with being broke when you make this affirmation.

- Write these affirmations on index cards and put them in places you regularly frequent. Stick some on your bathroom mirror and place some on your nightstand. You can even take a picture of your favorite affirmation and save it as your phone's lock screen wallpaper.

- Repeat your positive affirmations several times during the day—in the morning, midday, in the evening, before you go to bed and during moments of insecurity.

To create new beliefs and lasting thought patterns, your mind requires repetition. The repetition of affirmations enables them to go from being awkward statements to new beliefs. Real change happens when beliefs become internalized convictions. Think about it. Your negative self-talk wasn't formed the first time you told yourself you weren't good enough. You had to repeat this negative self-talk over and over again until it became an internalized truth. It's the same with bringing positivity into your life. With repetition and small tweaks in your behavior, the affirmations will start to sound more and more true. And the truer they sound, the more willing you will be to set aside your negative viewpoints to make room for these new positive beliefs.

NEGATIVE THOUGHT	POSITIVE AFFIRMATION
I am poor.	I am aligned with the energy of abundance.
I am so broke.	I am a magnet for money. Prosperity is drawn to me.
I'm terrible at managing my money.	I am in command of my money.
Everyone else is doing so much better than me.	I am moving at a pace that is right for me. My time is coming.
I'll never pay off my credit card debt.	I am developing a strong dedication to living a debt-free life.
Money goes out for me faster than it comes in.	I am starting to effortlessly resist spending money on things I don't need.

How Do Positive Affirmations Work?

Upon being introduced to positive affirmations a few years ago, I'll admit I dismissed them as being yet another ritual the super "woke" had put in place to sequester themselves from us "common" folk; however, I was wrong. It turns out, on a scientific level, positive affirmations do, in fact, work. And in the next few sections, I'll break down exactly why.

Our brains are equipped with a set of nuclei, or neural connections, called the reticular activating system (RAS). Its most significant function is the control of consciousness, especially the ability to deliberately focus on something. The RAS is why you're able to be at a coffee shop full of talking people, yet promptly snap to attention when the barista calls your name or something that sounds close to it. Thanks to the RAS, our brain can register what is pertinent to us based on our goals, interests, needs, and desires. The RAS takes this information and creates a filter for it. As you go through your day and your mind is presented with data, it sifts through the information and brings what it believes will be relevant to you to the forefront. This happens without you even noticing.[3]

Let's say you and a friend are walking down a busy street together. You're hungry, while your friend is in the mood to shop. As you both walk, you are going to see all the restaurants and no shopping stores. On the other hand, your friend is going to notice all the fabulous shopping stores and none of the restaurants. This is your RAS in action.

So how are positive affirmations and your reticular activating system correlated? When you commit to positive affirmations, it sends a message to your RAS that what you are affirming is vital to you. Your reticular activating system kicks in and notices different ways to help you realize what you are affirming. If you think you're terrible at managing your personal finances and can't move away from these thoughts, you'll remain bad at handling them. If you decide to stray away from these thoughts and begin affirming wealth into your life, your attention will be drawn to money-making and wealth-building opportunities.

Essentially, the RAS seeks information that validates your beliefs. It filters the world through the criteria you give it, with your beliefs playing a pivotal role in how this criteria is created. If you are affirming positivity and wealth into your life, the RAS is a godsend. But if you aren't and instead are stuck in a poverty mindset, your brain will look to other available influences and filters, such as subconscious fears and insecurities you haven't dealt with.

Affirmations Apply Just the Right Amount of Pressure

The other way affirmations work is by putting on the pressure. If you are affirming wealth but continually spend your money on frivolous items and make poor financial decisions, you're going to begin to feel uncomfortable. You will feel the difference between what you are affirming and the lifestyle you are living. You'll want to rid yourself of this discomfort, so you'll either stop saying the affirmations or begin to change your behavior so the affirmations can become your reality.

Conclusion

In this chapter, we covered the four components of a poverty mindset: negative perception, negative self-talk, playing the blame game, and constant complaining. To transition from a poverty mindset to one geared toward wealth, you will need to change your perception to see people and situations in a newer, more positive light. You will also need to stop blaming others for your plight in life by accepting responsibility and culpability for your actions and reactions. And finally, you'll need to go from being your biggest critic to your number one cheerleader.

My recommendation for jumpstarting this transition is to harness the power of positive affirmations. Positive affirmations allow you to clear out the negativity that has stifled and clouded your mind by helping you create new beliefs and thought patterns. When you first start off, it may seem weird saying all these nice and positive things to yourself. It may even feel gimmicky since you've probably spent much of your life viewing situations through a negative lens and thinking hurtful and unforgiving things about yourself. It's going to take a while to break the pattern of negative self-talk, negative perceptions, constant complaining, and playing the blame game.

During your wealth journey, you will undoubtedly have moments where you revert to these old habits. That is to be expected. The goal is not to be transformed into a perfect being but, rather, to allow more instances in your life where you view situations, people, and yourself in a newer, more positive light.

Activity

For this chapter's activity, we will be working on challenging your negative self-talk by being aware of it instead of shrugging it off. Plan a day where you consciously focus on your self-talk, and whenever you realize you're speaking to yourself negatively, write down your negative self-talk and ask yourself the following questions:

- What is the negative self-talk? What specifically am I saying?

- What feelings and behaviors does this negative dialogue cause?
- What will happen if I keep talking to myself this way?
- Does this negative dialogue help me reach my goals?

In addition to writing down your negative self-talk and questioning its validity, you could also jot down what a more confident, compassionate, positive, or even forgiving person would say to themselves instead. For example, if your negative self-talk is saying you don't have the skills to accomplish a task, think of a more forgiving thought, such as, *This is my first time doing this, so I'm going to do my best and use this as a learning experience.* If your negative self-talk is saying you don't have much of a future because of past mistakes, think of a more positive thought, such as such as, *I got off to a shaky start, but I'm getting better and better every day.*

By regularly challenging your self-talk, it will become easier to change it from negative to positive, or at least view things from a clearer perspective.

RULE #2

Change Your Relationship with Money for the Better

It was the summer of 2005. I was fifteen years old and tired of scraping together the measly fifteen-dollar weekly allowance my parents gave me, so I decided to launch a babysitting venture to bring in "real" money. With my mother's help, I took flyers I'd made on Microsoft Word and put them in mailboxes throughout our neighborhood. It took a few days, but eventually, I got a hit. Tax season was approaching, and my neighbor, who was a tax accountant, needed someone to watch her four kids. With no hesitation, I took the job. On my first payday, no sooner had my neighbor put a fresh, crisp wad of twenty- and fifty-dollar bills in my hand, was I at the mall blowing it on Justice, Juicy Couture, and Baby Phat outfits.

The response from my parents was swift. They let me keep the new outfits but opened a savings account for me at their credit union. All the money from my babysitting venture was to go untouched into this savings account.

"You need to save for a rainy day," they warned me.

But therein lay the problem. My parents were first-generation immigrants from Haiti who had migrated to the United States empty-handed for a fresh start. But somehow, their harrowing relationship with money, which had developed while living in a politically and financially unstable country, had managed to sneak in with them. Growing up, it felt like every day was a rainy day, and even when it wasn't raining, we were recovering from past rainy days or preparing for rainy days ahead. As a child, I watched my parents interact with money in this manner. When it was time for me to develop my relationship with money, I mimicked their behaviors and adopted their mindset.

My interactions with money from a young age centered around it being an incredibly scarce resource. To me, money represented survival; the more I had, the more equipped I would be for "rainy days." I believed you could never have enough money and held on to it super tight when I had it since I never internalized the feeling of monetary abundance. It took me several years to make this connection.

You see, we spend countless hours thinking of ways to make and spend money, but rarely do we think about how our relationships and mindsets toward money were formed. The reality is we have been hardwired from childhood to think about money in specific ways, including how we acquire, spend, and manage it. How we witnessed money being handled during our childhood by our parents, grandparents, and close relatives and how we organized this information shapes the complex relationship we have with it.

Shine a Light on Your Money Scripts

The complex relationships and beliefs we have surrounding money are called "money scripts." The concept of money scripts was developed by father and son duo Drs. Brad and Ted Klontz, pioneers in the emerging field of financial psychology. According to the duo, money scripts are unconscious financial beliefs developed early in our childhood that are passed from one generation to the next. Their research has identified four distinct money scripts: money avoidance, money worship, money status, and money vigilance.[4]

Money scripts drive financial behaviors and are associated with income, net worth, and debt. Beliefs, such as "More money, more problems," "I do not deserve a lot of money when others have less than me," "Money is power," and "Your net worth is your actual worth," all tie into money scripts formed due to experiences we viewed or felt in our childhood. Everyone has a money script, not just those with money problems. It's a good idea to know which money script you subscribe to, as this will allow you to have a better understanding of your mentality toward money and how you approach your finances.

Money Avoidance

Those who fall into the money avoidance script believe money is bad or they are undeserving of it. They associate money with emotions of anxiety, fear, and regret, and they correlate money and wealth with behaviors like greed and corruption. Money avoiders try not to think about money, ignore financial statements, enable others financially, give money away in an attempt to have as little as possible, and have difficulty managing and keeping a budget.

Money Worship

Those who fall into the money worship script believe money makes all things better. They think a pay raise or financial windfall will solve all their problems. They believe money brings prestige and joy. Those who hold this mindset are always in the pursuit of money and believe they can never have enough. In their pursuit of happiness, money worshippers tend to put work and money-making opportunities ahead of their family and other obligations.

Money Status

Those who fall into the money status script associate their self-worth with their bank account. They believe people are only as successful as the amount of money they earn and associate money with their overall sense of well-being. They often find themselves in an ongoing competition of acquiring more than those around them and may, at times, pretend to have more money than they actually have. They always want the newest and greatest items, as they associate it with a higher status.

Money Vigilance

Those who fall into the money vigilance script are watchful and mindful of their financial welfare. They believe in working hard, the importance of saving, and do not like to be given financial handouts. Their bills are paid on time and in full each month. When it comes to their financial status, earnings, and wealth, they are tight-lipped.

Some who subscribe to this money script have behaviors and habits that verge on obsession. It's healthy to budget so you can be on track to hit your financial goals, be financially prepared for emergencies, and stay in control of your finances; however, when your frugality affects relationships or the quality of your life because you refuse to part with money, that's a sign your money vigilance script may be getting the best of you. At this point, you're no longer frugal but, instead, have become what financial therapists call an "under spender."[5] Characteristics of an "under spender" are as follows:

- Neglecting necessary repairs and maintenance, such as getting a broken A/C fixed because you don't want to spend the money
- Having a robust savings account and little to no debt but constantly agonizing about money
- Avoiding essential health care because you don't want to deal with the copay
- Leaving an embarrassingly small tip for the sake of saving money
- Taking advantage of charitable services meant for people going through financial hardship, despite not facing any type of financial distress
- Haggling with a provider on their quality of service to see if you can get an item for free

This issue is agnostic of income. Some who underspend may make $800,000 a year, while others may make $50,000. Under spenders go without things they can afford because it pains them to part with their money. This causes them to not make use of their resources.

Challenge Your Money Script

Yes, money scripts are passed down from generation to generation, but that doesn't mean you're stuck with yours. According to the Klontz duo, money scripts are partial truths that, once identified, can be challenged and changed to interrupt damaging financial patterns and promote wealth.

Challenging the Money Avoidance Script

Whether you avoid money and your personal finances because you are experiencing financial stress or want to avoid the negative emotional associations you have with money, the money avoidance script can have severe implications on your financial health. Money avoiders looking to overcome this script should work to put financial rituals in place, such as a monthly personal finance date night or regularly scheduled meetings with a financial advisor.

In addition to putting financial rituals in place, those who subscribe to the money avoidance script need to work on disassociating the negative emotions they have toward money by thinking of the good. Take some time to create a list of ideas surrounding money and how it can be used for good, not only for you and your family but also for the rest of the world.

And finally, those who subscribe to this script need to face their personal finances head-on by setting and sticking to a budget. When creating a budget, identify a few financial goals and reward yourself when you reach them. Make sure your financial goals are achievable to prevent frustration.

Challenging the Money Worship Script

In the society we live in, money worship beliefs are prevalent and even admired. It's going to be challenging, but removing the association you've created between your self-worth and income is vital for your financial health, relationships, and bank account. The attachment money worshippers have developed between their self-worth and income sometimes manifests through random and extravagant purchases that result in buyer's remorse once the initial buzz wears off.

If you often find yourself making useless purchases and experiencing buyer's remorse, a good practice is to put some time between your impulse to buy something and pulling the trigger on the purchase by asking yourself the following questions:

- Why am I buying this item?
- Is there any type of peer pressure or social pressure surrounding this purchase?
- What do I prove by making this purchase?
- How does the item I'm looking to purchase fit into my lifestyle?
- Do I already own something that serves a comparable purpose?
- How does this item align with my values and needs?
- Can I afford to pay for this item in full right now?

After asking these questions, you might still end up making the purchase, but at least you've done the legwork to prevent it from being an impulsive purchase that results in buyer's remorse.

Money worshippers looking to conquer their script will also need to make time for loved ones. Unfortunately, attaching money to your happiness means you are continually working more hours to make more money to feel happier. Set specific times throughout the week for loved ones only. Block this time off on your calendar, turn your electronic devices off, and commit to being fully present during these moments.

And finally, to conquer this money script, money worshippers need to learn to give back. Money isn't the only source of joy. There is an immense amount of delight and an improved sense of self-esteem and self-worth that comes with giving. Allocate a portion of your monthly income to charity and thoughtful giving. Be sure this is budgeted and tracked, and do not fall into the trap of giving beyond your means.

Challenging the Money Vigilance Script

Those who subscribe to the money vigilance script find it difficult to embrace the concept of working hard and playing hard. Those looking to overcome this script need to learn to have fun with their money. One way to do this is by creating space in their budget with a "fun money" fund to enjoy the fruits of their labor. There's no point living a lifetime of scrimping and saving if you never allow yourself or your family to enjoy the money you've worked so hard for.

Also, subscribers of this script need to stop letting their financial fears and anxieties eat them alive. If your money vigilance script makes you constantly check your bank accounts, keeps you up at night, or gets in the way of other hobbies and activities you want to do, it's probably time for a change. Be deliberate about spending less time agonizing over your finances. If you spend an hour a day checking your bank accounts and keeping tabs on your financial progress and wealth goals, decrease it to forty-five minutes a day. Keep scaling back until you reach a healthy level.

Challenging the Money Status Script

The culture we live in tends to associate the state of one's finances with their social status. If you're looking to overcome the money status script, you need to understand your net worth is a part of you; however, it does not define you.

Money status seekers need to slow down before making purchases and come to terms with the fact that they sometimes buy the latest and greatest in an attempt to flash their "wealth." The ramifications of this have more than likely been detrimental for their pocketbooks. If you're looking to detach yourself from the money status script, ask yourself the following questions before making purchases:

- Why am I buying this item?
- What emotion does purchasing this item fulfill for me?
- How long do these emotions and feelings last?
- Do I have the money to pay for this item?
- What do I prove by making this purchase?
- How will I feel about this purchase in the long run?

When answering these questions, challenge your logic and dig deep. You may initially go into a store thinking the item you are buying is essential, but after defying your logic and digging deeper, you may begin to realize you're buying the item to appear impressive or cool. Before buying an item, envision the emotions you might experience when you make the purchase—enthusiasm, fulfillment, or even pride. Ask yourself: Is there a better way to feel this emotion without continuing with the purchase?

And finally, someone trying to detach themselves from the money status script needs to understand that wealth encompasses more than their finances. Wealth also encompasses their health. The strong drive for monetary success accompanied by the money status script means those who subscribe to this script tend to suffer from workaholism. Workaholism can destroy your relationships, as well as your physical and mental well-being. Make time for what matters most, whether it be earmarking time in your calendar to work out, cook healthy meals, or spend time with family and friends.

Improving Your Relationship with Money

In addition to shining a light on your money scripts and challenging them, there are additional steps you can take to improve your relationship with money, such as taking some time to think about how your money scripts were formed and forgiving yourself for past financial mistakes.

Think about How Your Money Scripts Were Formed

To better understand how your money scripts were formed, recall your earliest childhood memories you have surrounding money:

- What is your most joyful childhood memory involving money?

- What is your most unpleasant childhood memory involving money?
- Describe your housing situation when you were younger. Did you live in a house or an apartment?
- Did you grow up in a single-income or dual-income household?
- What kind of cars did your family have? Did you have one at all?
- Were your parents/grandparents spenders or savers?
- Was there an abundance or scarcity mindset in your household?
- Did you go on family vacations?
- Did you eat at restaurants a lot?
- What kind of clothes did you wear?
- Growing up, did you have an allowance?
- At what age did you begin working? Did the compensation from your job go toward your family's household bills?
- Did you have to pay for things, or did your parents take care of it all?
- In what ways were you required to contribute to your household as a teen?

Remember, our present-day financial behaviors are rooted in the behaviors we witnessed in our caretakers as a child. And our caretakers' financial behaviors stem from the behaviors they encountered as children. It's a cycle. Dig as deep as you can into this cycle by talking to your caretakers about their money beliefs and earliest money memories. Go back as many generations as you can. By understanding how your family's money scripts were formed, your money beliefs and financial behaviors will begin to make more sense.

Forgive Yourself

You've probably made poor financial decisions that haunt you to this day due to the combination of behaviors and patterns you observed as a child. To advance on your wealth journey, you need to forgive yourself for these mistakes. With the financial skills, tools, and understanding you had at the time, you did your best. You can't change the debts you've incurred, the bills you've neglected, or your lack of savings. What you can do now is accept what has been done and promise to do better in the future. Everyone has made mistakes. Mistakes propel us forward. They are a crucial part of one's story, and only you get to determine how the story ends.

Claiming "I forgive myself" is a start, but that isn't going to get you far. To forgive yourself, you must *want* to move forward. Some people don't believe they are worthy and deserving of wealth and prosperity, so they wallow in guilt instead of forgiving themselves for past financial mistakes. Do you believe you are worthy and deserving of wealth? If not, why?

Think about the emotions associated with the financial mistakes you've made. To forgive yourself, you must let go of these emotions. Do you feel guilty every time you think about your credit card debt? Why do you feel this guilt? Get to the root of the emotions associated with your financial mistakes so you can let them go. Don't deny your mistakes or attempt to place the blame on others. If you do, you'll find yourself making the same mistakes repeatedly because you never accepted responsibility.

Whatever happened has happened. Let go of the past and commit to a better and brighter future. Every day is an opportunity to make better choices. As with any journey, your wealth journey is going to have ups and downs. You may have a period when you go months making aggressive payments toward your debt, hit a roadblock, and cut back on payments for a month or two because of life. Adapt, refocus, and instead of wallowing in guilt, think about how far you've come and how much further you will go tomorrow.

Conclusion

Our relationship with money was formed based on how we witnessed our caretakers handling it during childhood. These observations have led to us developing money scripts. Although money scripts develop in our formative years, they are not rigid, meaning they can evolve and change as we journey through life. Whether you subscribe to a money avoidance, money worship, money status, or money vigilance script, it's imperative you get to the root of your relationship with money. Getting to the heart of your money relationship will allow you to better understand your financial behaviors and put a more strategic financial plan in place.

If you're reading this book, you've likely made financial mistakes. You more than likely made these mistakes due to a combination of behaviors you witnessed as a child and the little financial skills, tools, and understanding you've been equipped with. Instead of dwelling on how much debt you could have paid off or how much money you could have saved if you started earlier, focus on the present. Forgive yourself for past mistakes and make a promise to do better moving forward.

Activity

Regardless of the money script you subscribe to, if you want to build wealth, you're going to need to develop a healthy relationship with your money. To establish a healthy relationship with money, you need to make time for it.

For this chapter's activity, you'll be doing just that by having a personal finance date night. During this session, you'll comb through your bank accounts and recent purchases, reevaluate your long- and short-term financial goals to stay on track, identify trends, and nip lousy behavior in the bud. Below is a list of items to review during your personal finance date night:

- Savings account balance(s)
- Credit card balance(s)
- Investment account balance(s)
- Total thirty-day spending
- Budgeted vs. actual spending
- Steps made toward long- and short-term financial goals
- Bills paid
- Upcoming bills

A personal finance date night doesn't need to be complicated; it just needs to be routine. It's going to take a few tries to find a cadence that works best for you, but the more you do it, the more of a habit it will become. A few tips for making the most of your finance date night are as follows:

1. **Block it off on your calendar.** A finance date night should be a priority, not a spur-of-the-moment activity. It should be a scheduled, monthly session on your calendar.

2. **Make it exciting.** You shouldn't dread having a personal finance date night. Instead, you should be looking forward to it. Order takeout from your favorite restaurant (if your budget allows it), munch on your favorite snacks, or uncork your favorite bottle of wine.
3. **It's OK if you get triggered.** Talking and even thinking about money brings up intense emotions for some people. The purpose of a personal finance date night isn't to dwell on past financial mistakes. It is a time-bound, safe space you've created to honestly and openly review your finances. Undoubtedly, you'll go over budget, miss payments, and fall short of your goals from time to time. Your personal finance date night shouldn't be used as an opportunity to cast judgment or get emotional but, rather, to reset and readjust strategically.
4. **Envision your future.** A lot of people talk about being wealthy, but I wonder how many people envision it. During your finance date nights, don't just go through the motions of mundanely sorting through your finances; think about your wealth goals and feel them. Allow yourself to become excited! If your goal is to pay off all your debt, envision how accomplished you're going to feel when you make that last debt payment. If your goal is to save enough money to travel the world, get excited thinking of all the places you're going to go.

RULE # 3

Establish Financial Independence by Living Beneath Your Means

It starts slowly. Your budget for dining out is fifty dollars a week, and you typically bring your lunch to work three out of five days during the workweek, but things have been hectic lately, so you grab lunch with coworkers at a restaurant near the office every day. You end up completely blowing your weekly dining out budget and spending $150 versus your budgeted fifty dollars. The next week is even more chaotic. You manage to bring your lunch to work every day of the week but grab a latte and a muffin at the coffee shop near the office every morning. Once again, you completely blow your dining out budget and spend ninety dollars that week versus the budgeted fifty dollars.

Living above your means begins as a slow leak, but like all leaks, once you put a bucket under them, you're surprised at how much has accumulated. It starts with you spending more in certain categories, such as entertainment, food, gas, etc., without intending to. You convince yourself you'll compensate for this overspending by spending less in other categories. If you've spent too much money dining out, you convince yourself you'll cut down on your entertainment expenses. If you've spent too much money shopping for clothes, you convince yourself you'll be more price conscious when you shop for groceries. Unfortunately, this compromise never happens.

Worse still, you may compensate for your overspending by dipping into your savings account. But this begins a vicious cycle of transferring a few hundred dollars to your savings account when you get paid, only to move it back to your checking account in small increments when you're running low on funds until there was no point in attempting to save in the first place.

Sometimes living above your means doesn't involve small expenses that creep in but, instead, prioritizing lifestyle choices that don't match your bank account. All your colleagues are driving luxury cars, so you decide you should drive one too, but now, you're stuck with a shiny new car, inflated insurance costs, and maintenance fees you can barely afford. Or you've had a quarter-life crisis and decided you want to "experience more things," and a massive case of FOMO (fear of missing out) sets in. You're taking vacations to remote islands because everyone on Instagram, Facebook, and TikTok is doing so. Yet, you can barely afford to do any activities or live like a local on said vacation because you didn't adequately budget for the trip, blew your savings on the flight, and maxed out a credit card for the hotel.

There are long-term consequences associated with living above your means, especially if you are looking to build wealth and obtain financial freedom. In this chapter, we will thoroughly examine these consequences and provide step-by-step instructions on how to break this lifestyle pattern so you'll have room in your finances to make the necessary financial investments for your future.

What Happens When You Live Above Your Means?

Unmanageable bills and living expenses, creeping credit card debt, limited progress toward your wealth goals, and an inability to reign in your spending habits. Sounds like a nightmare, right? Unfortunately, this is just a sample of what your life looks like when you're living above your means. In the next few sections, I'll go over some of the top consequences of living above your means.

Consequence 1: Unmanageable Bills and Living Expenses

As hinted earlier, living above your means doesn't necessarily equate to small, mindless, and compounding day-to-day expenses. Sometimes living above your means looks like making significant lifestyle choices that propel you into a cycle of living paycheck to paycheck.

The easiest way to find yourself living above your means is by being stuck in an expensive housing situation. It is recommended that no more than thirty percent of your annual gross income goes toward your housing. For renters, this percentage should include utilities, and for homeowners, the thirty percent should include homeownership costs, such as interest, property taxes, and maintenance.

Using this reference, someone whose gross annual income is $55,000 should try to keep their monthly housing costs around $1,375. But let's say you decide to throw this recommendation to the wind and enter into an expensive housing situation where you're paying around $1,900 a month. At a glance, this isn't a big deal. After all, it's only $525 more a month.

But the reality is someone making $55,000 simply cannot handle having that much of their income going solely toward their housing expenses. This $1,900 is an unmanageable amount that is going to cut into other areas of their life, especially their ability to comfortably pay for other bills and living expenses.

Consequence 2: Limited Progress toward Wealth Goals

The extra $525 you can barely afford for your housing costs has long-term repercussions. That is $525 you aren't able to contribute toward paying off debt, saving for retirement, or simply putting in a bank account to prepare for rainy days. One of the fundamentals of building wealth is sacrificing in the short term to make room for long-term prosperity. But because you're living above your means, paying $525 more than you should toward your housing costs, you aren't able to make this sacrifice.

Consequence 3: No Control of Your Spending Habits

Many believe they'll be able to manage their finances better when they reach a certain income level. This isn't the case most of the time, as your lifestyle will rise to meet the new income you've attained because you haven't fine-tuned your spending. You don't suddenly acquire the ability to handle money by having more of it. Financial literacy isn't a side effect of having more money.

If someone making $55,000 annually who pays $1,900 in

housing costs were to get a promotion or pay raise where they're suddenly making $70,000 annually, they'd probably use this income increase to justify upgrading to more expensive housing. This decision would force them even deeper into the cycle of living paycheck to paycheck and above their means.

Consequence 4: Creeping Credit Card Debt

In the example above, where someone's housing cost is $525 more than it should be, the problem is more profound than merely paying an absurd amount for rent. The reality is unfortunate financial mistakes don't live in a vacuum; amid poor financial decisions, life still continues.

When your housing cost is $525 more than it should be, this severely limits the amount you're able to set aside in a savings account, which causes small emergencies to become credit-card-worthy events. Run over a nail and need to get your tires patched? You end up reaching for your credit card. Have a medical bill that is higher than expected? You end up reaching for your credit card. Eventually, you look up, and you've amassed a ton of credit card debt in an attempt to make ends meet, all because you got into a housing situation that was $525 more than you could afford.

Benefits of Living Beneath One's Means

Living beneath your means is a discipline where you decide to spend less than you make. Just because you have money doesn't mean you should spend it. Setting a portion of your income aside to pay down debt, invest, and save for retirement has positive benefits, not only for your future but for the generations that will come after you. Living beneath your means is the foundation of wealth and allows for the following:

- Paying down debt, such as student loans, medical bills, credit cards
- Building up an emergency savings fund
- Contributing money to sinking funds
- Contributing to a 401(k)
- Financial liquidity
- Less stress
- Financial confidence and pride

How to Start Living Beneath Your Means

We've described the consequences of living above your means and how the discipline of living beneath them allows you to take the necessary steps toward building wealth. But now, you're probably wondering, *How do I go about practicing this discipline?* To live beneath your means, you need to set a budget and stick to it. In the following pages, we will focus on how to live beneath your means by evaluating your financial goals, tracking your income, assessing your spending habits, setting a budget, and holding yourself accountable.

There are various budgeting methodologies out there. The one you end up using boils down to whether your end goal is to curb spending, pay down debt, build your savings, etc. For this book's purpose, we will be using my favorite method, the zero-based budgeting method.

The zero-based budgeting method encourages you to use

every penny of your monthly income with the goal of giving every cent a purpose. With this method, you allocate all of your money to your living expenses, savings, investment accounts, and debt payments. The goal is to have your income minus these expenses equal zero at the end of the month. If the end of the month rolls around and you have $400 left over, you aren't done with the budget yet. You need to find somewhere for that money to go (preferably putting it toward an extra debt payment, using it to fund investments, stashing it away in an emergency savings fund, or contributing it to a sinking fund).

Creating a Budget Using the Zero-Based Budgeting Method

STEP 1: SET FINANCIAL GOALS.

We all have dreams for the future, most of which require money and planning to come to fruition. Perhaps you want to pay off all your credit cards, backpack through Europe, pad your emergency savings fund, contribute aggressively to your retirement plan, or start saving to send your child to college. To bring these dreams to fruition, you must set clear financial goals. Before creating your budget, think of a few financial goals you'd like to accomplish. Use the SMART method of goal-setting to ensure your success.

How to Set SMART Goals

SMART is a well-established methodology used to plan and accomplish goals. Most of the time, our goals are too vague, which is why we have trouble reaching them. Setting SMART goals allows you to clarify your ideas and focus your efforts.

With SMART goals, your plans go from being distant dreams to your reality by embodying five distinct traits: Specific, Measurable, Achievable, Relevant, and Time-Bound (hence the acronym "SMART").

- **Specific:** The goal should be clear and have a highly specific endpoint. "To get richer" is not a precise or clear goal, but "to pay for seventy-five percent of my child's college tuition" is.
- **Measurable:** For your goal to be practical, it needs to be calculable. You need to be able to track and measure your progress accurately.
- **Achievable:** Setting achievable goals can be tricky. You want to push yourself, but if you set a goal that is not achievable, it will sap your motivation, causing you to struggle. Use your income (and expected income) to set your goals for the future. Don't count on winning the lottery, luck, donations, help from others, or hope to achieve what you want.
- **Relevant:** The goals you make should be pertinent to your life and benefit you directly. Just because all of your friends are traveling doesn't mean you have to start saving to travel. You might hate traveling and instead want to save money to buy equipment to start a band or pursue a hobby.
- **Time-Bound:** Setting a time frame for your goals keeps you on track and helps quantify your goals even further. An example of a time-bound goal is "I want to pay

off my Capital One and Macy's credit cards in twelve months."

After you've set your financial goals using the SMART method, it's time to take the next step toward creating your budget: tracking and recording all sources of income.

STEP 2: TRACK AND RECORD ALL SOURCES OF INCOME.

Budgeting is about making the best use of your income, so you need to know exactly how much money you have coming in. Gather bank statements, pay stubs, and any information that provides details of your income from the past two months. If you are self-employed, have a side hustle, or have additional income sources outside of your primary job, be sure to accurately record these sources of income. After you've gathered all your income information, tally it into one average monthly amount.

STEP 3: TRACK, RECORD, AND EVALUATE YOUR EXPENSES.

Account for your expenses from the past two months. If, for some reason, you don't have access to your previous two months' expenses, plan two months where you diligently save your receipts and track all expenses so you can take part in this exercise. If you use a debit or credit card, this exercise will be easy, as you can utilize your bank's mobile app or bank statements to see your transactions and their associated date and amount. During this step, create a worksheet where you break down all your expenses into two categories: essential and non-essential.

Essential expenses are expenses that must be paid each month.

Examples of essential expenses include housing (whether it be rent or mortgage), groceries, child support, daycare, utilities, car note, car insurance, gas, health care (including medications), debt payments on your student loans, credit card payments, as well as your contributions toward your emergency savings fund, sinking funds, and investing accounts.

Non-essential expenses are items you spend money on each month that are not crucial. These expenses are wants, not needs. Examples of expenses and bills in this category include gym memberships, charitable donations, dining out, vacations, movies, and entertainment subscriptions, such as Spotify or Netflix, etc.

Your first time going through this exercise is going to leave you shocked. You may not realize that the bulk of your expenses are in the non-essential category, or you may be shocked to find you're spending substantially more on certain items and experiences than you thought. After you've gathered all your expenses and separated them according to whether they are essential or non-essential, tally them into one average monthly expense amount.

Step 4: Decide how much you want to contribute to wealth-building activities.

Keeping in mind the SMART financial goals you've set, your average monthly income, and your monthly expenses, decide how much money you want to contribute each month toward wealth-building activities. If you want to build up your emergency savings fund and you've set a financial goal of saving $7,000 in twelve months, you'll need to set aside $584 monthly. If you want to get rid of debt and you've set a goal to pay off $2,200 in credit card debt in twelve months, you'll need to contribute at least $184 a month toward this debt. Depending on your monthly income and expenses, you may be able to tackle both of these goals, or you may have to narrow it down to one.

Step 5: Prioritize expenses.

Prioritize your expenses by importance. You've already gotten started on this step by separating your expenses based on whether they are non-essential or essential. During this step, make sure you keep your financial goals top of mind. If your goal is to pay off a few of your credit cards, you'll need to prioritize your credit card payments over non-essential expenses, such as entertainment or dining out. A rule of thumb is to prioritize essential expenses first, followed by the amounts you want to allocate to your wealth-building initiatives. Then, finish by adding in your non-essential expenses.

Step 6: Determine where you stand.

The ultimate goal with the zero-based budgeting method is to be in a situation where your income minus expenses equals zero. This means all of your income is budgeted for a specific expense or wealth-building objective. If, after prioritizing your expenses, you determine your income is higher than your expenses, congratulations, you live beneath your means. This means you can reallocate additional money toward saving, paying off debt, or investing. But if you determine you're spending more than you're making, it's time to do some ruthless cutting so you have room to save, aren't living paycheck to paycheck, and can make the necessary contributions toward your financial goals to build wealth.

Step 7: Cut and trim expenses.

The best place to start when cutting and trimming expenses is the non-essential expense category. Can you skip movie night in favor of a movie at home? Can you limit yourself to dining out once a week, with a weekly spending limit of thirty dollars, and cook meals at home instead? Play around and adjust the numbers you've tracked to see how much money is freed from cutting and trimming your non-essential expenses.

Having trouble wrapping your mind around cutting and trimming expenses? Below are four non-essential everyday expenditures you may be spending money on each month that quickly add up:

1. **Daily coffee purchases:** A latte costs around four dollars. If you stop by your local coffee shop every morning to buy a latte, you'll have spent close to $1,500 on lattes annually.
2. **Gym memberships:** Assuming a gym membership costs one hundred dollars a month, you can save $1,200 a year by cutting this expense. If your gym membership is valuable to you and you faithfully use it, by all means, keep it! If not, subscribing to a fitness channel on YouTube, hitting up your community recreation center, or joining a local sports team can put money back in your pocket.
3. **Happy hours:** After a crazy and stress-filled workweek, it's nice to unwind and meet up with friends and coworkers for drinks. But if you buy two twelve-dollar

cocktails each week, you're spending $1,248 a year on happy hours alone.

4. **Takeout/fast food:** The average American household spends about $3,000 a year dining out. Are you thinking there's no way you could spend that much on food? Let's take another look. You might only spend ten dollars a meal when you dine out, but if you go out for lunch Monday through Friday for a year (which is on the low end), this quickly adds up to fifty dollars weekly. If you spend fifty dollars a week on restaurant food, you'll have spent $2,600 per year.

If you've already adjusted your spending in the non-essential category and still need to cut and trim to get to zero, it's time to evaluate your essential expenses. It is essential to have a roof over your head, but what would the numbers look like if you got a roommate or put one of your guest rooms on Airbnb? Medication is also essential, but what would the numbers look like if you switched from name-brand to generic prescriptions?

While doing this exercise, you'll find it's harder to cut and trim expenses in your essential category than it is for your non-essential expenses. You can easily cut down on the number of happy hours you go to each week with little repercussions; however, it would be ill-advised for you to cut down on your medications. Or it might be next to impossible to cut down on your monthly car note, as you're probably locked into a long-term payment plan. When it comes to cutting and trimming expenses in the essential category, I recommend the following:

- Calling your service providers, i.e., car insurance, cell phone, etc., to see if there are bundles or promotions they can put your services on to lower the monthly cost

- Cooking the majority of your meals at home
- Using coupons and incorporating meatless meals to save on food costs
- Putting your bills on autopay to take advantage of most providers' discounts for this payment type
- Buying generic instead of name-brand items to trim costs
- Exercising regularly and implementing a healthier diet to cut down on your healthcare costs
- Cutting off lights and unplugging appliances when not in use
- Keeping the tires on your automobile inflated to the optimal PSI to ensure you are maxing out your gas mileage
- Carpooling to reduce the wear and tear on your vehicle and save on gas costs
- Lowering the temperature on your hot water heater
- Shopping for groceries at a farmer's market versus large-chain grocery stores

Trimming and cutting your expenses does not mean you have to give up everything you enjoy. Instead, it means prioritizing certain expenses while keeping your long-term financial goals in mind. You want to be purposeful with your money and use it as a tool to get you where you want to be financially.

Try not to trim and cut too much, as this might lead to the feeling of deprivation, which could have negative repercussions. Forcing yourself to feel financially deprived is like being on a restrictive diet; eventually, you will come off the diet and binge. Even worse, the results will be temporary. Living beneath your means and budgeting is not a one-time fad or experiment but, rather, a lifestyle.

Step 8: Set your budget.

You're now ready to set your budget. Tally up your trimmed essential and non-essential expenses and wealth-building contributions. This is now your monthly budget!

Step 9: Re-evaluate.

A budget is pointless if it isn't adhered to. After setting your budget, you should perform a weekly audit of your budgeted spending and actual spending to see how well or poorly you've done. While examining your actual versus budgeted spending, ask yourself the following questions:

- How realistic is my budget?
- What's the difference between my planned expenses and my actual expenses?
- In what areas or categories did I overspend?
- In what areas or categories did I spend less than what I budgeted?

After a few months, you can transition from a weekly audit to a monthly one. You may think once you've set your budget, you're now locked in and ready to go on your path to financial freedom and wealth. Unfortunately, this isn't the case. Living beneath your means is a lifestyle change and a huge undertaking. You're bound to fall off the wagon a few times. When this happens, don't beat yourself up. Instead, refocus and readjust. Here are a couple tips for sticking to your budget:

- Set up your banking app so you get a balance reminder each morning. This allows you to start your day knowing the exact state your finances are in.
- Set up your banking app to get a reminder once your account balance is below a certain threshold. This will allow you to reevaluate spending habits and hit the brakes on your spending if needed.

Conclusion

Living above one's means can happen to anyone; in fact, it's typically a period of living above one's means that inspires most to get their finances in order. There are innumerable benefits associated with cutting back on your spending and living beneath your means. The liquidity garnered from living beneath one's means affords them the ability to partake in more strategic and profitable wealth-building activities, such as investing, buying stocks and bonds, starting businesses, and purchasing property.

By setting a budget and consistently monitoring your spending, you can begin living beneath your means to take the first steps toward financial independence and wealth.

Activity

To effectively budget, you must separate your wants from your needs. Many have mistakenly spent their whole lives categorizing certain items as "needs" when they're really "wants" they've conditioned themselves to believe they can't live without. There's a fuzzy, emotionally drawn line between wants and needs that must be clearly redrawn for one to begin budgeting effectively.

For this chapter's activity, we will be going through a "wants" versus "needs" exercise. To partake in this exercise, save two weeks' worth of receipts for every transaction you make, whether it be your morning coffee run, groceries, prescriptions, furniture, mortgage, rent, takeout, utilities, etc. Take two envelopes and label one "wants" and the other "needs." At the end of the two weeks, sort through all your receipts and place them into what you believe is the corresponding envelope. At first glance, this seems like a straightforward activity, but as you go through the exercise, you'll quickly learn it isn't.

Despite living in the twenty-first century where the internet is seen as a "need," it's actually a "want." The only scenarios where your home internet would be a need is if you're running a business in your home or furthering your education, but let's be honest, for the majority of us, this isn't the case. Your smartphone, cable television, media subscriptions, such as HBO Now or Netflix, luxury face creams, and salon-grade deep conditioner are all wants, not needs. These items are not necessary for you to live; you could survive without them.

When you analyze your grocery bill, you'll notice it's a combination of wants and needs. You need a sufficient combination of fruits, vegetables, dairy, whole grains, poultry, meat, fish, legumes, and eggs to live; however, you *want* yogurt-covered pretzels, sunflower seeds, and gourmet popcorn. Let's not forget upscale varieties of food many attempt to pass off as needs. Your body needs adequate amounts of protein to thrive, but lobster tails and wagyu steak are a want. Likewise, bread is a need, but herb-infused focaccia garnished with rosemary, sundried tomatoes, and mozzarella is a want.

There's nothing wrong with having internet, buying salon-grade deep conditioner, eating herb-infused focaccia, and enjoying lobster tails. The purpose of this activity is not to shame you, rather it is to illustrate how much of your spending goes toward wants instead of needs.

People don't like to budget because they feel powerless with their money. They feel as if they barely have enough money to cover basics, such as rent, utilities, and groceries, so the idea of cutting and pruning expenses to make room for wealth-building activities, such as investing, saving, and paying off debt, seems far-fetched. This activity shows how much power and control you have over your money. If you're spending the bulk of your money on wants and non-essential expenses, you can easily choose not to buy those items and strategically divert your money toward a wealth-building activity.

The truth of the matter is budgeting is not just about slashing expenses and crunching numbers; it's about taking the aspects of your life you value and aligning your spending with them. You are not powerless with your money. Whether you have five dollars to your name or a million, your money has weight and impact; you're just using it ineffectively. Budgeting will change this.

RULE #4

Plan for the Future by Putting Financial Buffers in Place

My first car was a Hyundai Accent that I did a terrible job maintaining. On average, I went in for an oil change once a year, got it washed every other year, and one time, I might have accidentally put diesel in it instead of regular gas. The car reciprocated my nonchalant energy surrounding its maintenance and routinely failed on me. It was almost as if Bernadette, which I affectionately called her, was using those moments to teach me a lesson. If I remember correctly, it was the summer of 2012 when Bernadette taught me the mother of all lessons.

I was driving back home from a business trip when she stalled on the side of the highway. I had the car towed to the nearest repair shop, only to be given devastating news: A specific part needed to be ordered for the repair, and the whole ordeal, including labor, was going to cost $2,000. With no hesitation, I charged the $2,000 to one of my credit cards, but therein lay a problem: I was underwater financially, living paycheck to paycheck, and nowhere in the foreseeable future was I going to be able to pay the balance off. The card sat with the $2,000 balance for months, accruing late fees and interest, until the account was eventually turned over to collections. Two years later, after I was in a better financial state and had somewhat gotten a handle on my finances, I was able to muster up the courage to call the debt collector the account was assigned to and pay the balance off.

The situation I was in isn't too far from what many experience when they're faced with an emergency or unexpected expenses. The reality is the majority of people would have to either sell something, get help from family and friends, or go into debt to cover the cost of a sudden emergency expense. The good news? This situation can be avoided through the use of financial buffers. In this chapter, we will be discussing the financial buffers you should put in place for rainy days. Specifically, we will be discussing emergency savings funds, sinking funds, and cash cushions, highlighting their different purposes and the role they play in your wealth journey.

What Is an Emergency Savings Fund?

An emergency savings fund is a savings account that's set aside to cover emergency or unforeseen expenses, such as the following:

- **A surprise medical emergency:** A trip to the emergency room can create severe financial strain, especially if you are uninsured. And don't think you're off the hook if you're insured. Even with health insurance, you'll still need to pay the deductible and copay associated with the care you receive.

- **Unexpected and urgent home repairs:** If your home is damaged via a natural disaster, your insurance may pay for repairs, but you'll need to come out of pocket for the deductible, which can range from $500 to $1000. Not to mention, insurance doesn't cover everything. Your home may incur damage that isn't covered by your home insurance policy.
- **Job loss:** If you lose your job, you will have several bills and expenses that will need to be paid despite not receiving a regular and consistent paycheck.
- **Unanticipated travel:** An unanticipated event, like a sudden death in your family, could force you to purchase a last-minute plane ticket at an excessively high cost.
- **Emergency pet care:** On a day-to-day basis, the cost of owning a pet is pretty low, but would you be prepared to pay thousands of dollars if your cat or dog needed emergency surgery?

Having money set aside in an emergency savings fund can prevent you from turning to high-interest debt, like credit cards and payday loans, during times of crisis. It also prevents you from relying on family and friends or dipping into your 401(k).

If faced with a $500 emergency expense, the vast majority would not have the funds to cover it. Unfortunately, emergencies happen all the time and can be quite costly. Having an emergency savings fund is critical to the financial security of your family. You or a family member may get sick and have an ambulance bill you must deal with despite having health insurance, or you may have an unexpected car repair bill you have to cover. An emergency savings fund provides you with the reassurance of knowing you have something you can fall back on during rainy days.

How Much Should You Set Aside in Your Emergency Savings Fund?

For an emergency savings fund, it is recommended to have three to six months of expenses saved, with the ideal amount leaning toward six months. For example, if your monthly expenses total $4,000, you should have six months of expenses saved, which would have you at $24,000 set aside in an emergency savings fund.

Everyone's monthly financial obligations are unique, and your emergency savings fund will reflect this. Some may have low monthly expenses, no debt, or income from a partner they can rely on if a catastrophe or job loss were to occur. Someone in this boat would have a much lower amount in their emergency savings fund than a single person living off freelance gigs. Those in the latter example would need to have a heftier amount stashed away in their emergency savings fund.

When considering the amount of money to have in your emergency savings fund, you should start by calculating critical expenses that would still need to be paid despite facing a major catastrophe, such as:

- Housing
- Food
- Health care (insurance, prescriptions, routine medical visits, etc.)
- Utilities

- Transportation
- Personal expenses
- Debt (minimum payment amounts)

You don't need to include the expenses for anything you'd cut from your budget in the event of a job loss or significant catastrophe. Examples of expenses you can exclude from your emergency savings fund estimates are as follows:

- Entertainment
- Dining out
- Non-essential shopping
- Vacations

How Do You Get Started with an Emergency Savings Fund?

To get started with an emergency savings fund, you first need to understand that something is better than nothing. On average, most emergency savings funds are stocked with, at minimum, $10,000, which is an intimidating amount, especially when you are first starting out on your wealth journey. Don't panic. You don't need to come up with $10,000 overnight. You can build up to it by stashing away smaller amounts regularly, like every week or every paycheck. If you keep it up, you'll eventually reach your goal. The important thing is you start saving something.

For instance, let's say you set aside fifty dollars a week in an emergency savings fund. At the end of two years, you could have $5,200 saved. Increase this amount to seventy-five dollars a week, and your savings could grow to $7,800. Make it one hundred dollars a week, and you'll see an even more significant amount saved: $10,400. Additional ways to get started with an emergency savings fund are as follows:

- **Split your check:** Have a percentage or a specific amount of your paycheck direct deposited into your savings account each pay period.
- **Get in on the gig economy:** A side gig job, such as driving for Uber or Lyft or selling services on Fiverr, is a great way to bring in additional income earmarked solely for your emergency savings fund.
- **Try apps, like Qapital or Digit:** Digit analyzes your spending and automatically saves the perfect amount every day so you don't have to think about it. Qapital moves money from your checking account to a separate Qapital account when specific rules are triggered.
- **Save your tax refund:** Saving your tax refund can be an easy way to boost your emergency stash. When you file your taxes, have your refund deposited directly into the account where you store your emergency savings fund.
- **Strategically slash expenses:** Cut an expense, such as your gym membership or premium cable subscription, and have the former bill amount automatically transferred to your savings account on the date you would have paid that bill each month.
- **Sell your clutter:** Go through every room in your home and identify items you no longer use or need. Sell these items on eBay or Craigslist to put a few more dollars into your emergency savings fund.

Stopping Yourself from Dipping into Your Emergency Savings Fund

Building up your emergency savings fund is hard, and maintaining it is an even more daunting feat. If you feel you're always inclined to use money from your emergency savings fund or find you're always having to replenish the account, consider these three questions before dipping into your fund for an expense.

Question 1: How urgent is the emergency?

Is the "emergency" an event that can be held off until your next paycheck, or does it need to occur and be paid for immediately? If your car breaks down and is rendered useless, that would be considered an emergency event that would need to occur and be paid for immediately; however, routine car maintenance, such as getting new brake pads or tires, oil changes, etc., are not expenses that should be funded by your emergency savings. As a car owner, you know these expenses will come up during the year, so you should save up for them ahead of time and schedule them for when you have money on hand without having to dip into your emergency savings fund.

Question 2: Is it truly an emergency?

To prevent yourself from spending your emergency savings fund on frivolous items and experiences, you need to make sure you understand what constitutes an emergency. The following may seem obvious, but they are not emergencies that warrant dipping into your emergency savings fund:

- Black Friday shopping
- Christmas shopping
- Your favorite store having a sale, no matter how steep the discount or enticing the offer
- A travel deal posted by your preferred airline
- A life event you knew was coming up that you failed to prepare for

To ensure you understand what events warrant dipping into your emergency savings fund, generate a list of what you consider an emergency. This way, you won't feel hesitant to use your fund if any of these situations ever occur.

Bonus tip: To prevent yourself from impulsively transferring money from your savings to your checking account for "emergencies" that aren't really an emergency, consider housing your emergency savings fund in an account that is separate from the one linked to your checking account.

Question 3: Does the benefit of using the money outweigh the cost?

With each "emergency" that comes up, you need to determine if using your emergency savings fund is worthwhile. The benefit of using your emergency savings fund is being able to easily cover an emergency expense without slipping into debt. Unfortunately, this comes at a cost. Emergencies happen all the time. You may be fortunate to use your emergency savings fund for one expense, but it may be so significant that it completely depletes your fund, leaving you with nothing when the next emergency strikes.

Storing Your Emergency Savings Fund

With an emergency savings fund, four essentials should be kept in mind when it comes to storing it. Your emergency savings fund should be stored in an account that is low risk, insured, liquid, and easily accessible. It's not a good idea to put your rainy day funds in high-risk investments, such as stocks, that might incur significant losses. It doesn't matter how much money you've saved today if it's not available when you need it due to a market downturn. Instead, opt for low-risk accounts. Checking, savings, and money market accounts and certificates of deposit are a few examples of low-risk options for storing an emergency savings fund.

Make sure the bank you store your emergency savings fund in is FDIC insured. With FDIC insurance, bank balances up to $250,000 are insured by the Federal Deposit Insurance Corporation, which is backed by the United States government. The FDIC steps in and makes sure you get your money back if a bank goes out of business.

Banks are not mandated to be FDIC insured. Recently, several startups have released banking products that are not covered by FDIC insurance. These banking products offer exorbitantly higher interest rates than traditional and online banks have provided in the past, with perks, such as low fees and no minimum account balances. Unfortunately, these perks are all in vain if your money isn't insured. You can determine if a financial institution is FDIC insured by visiting the FDIC website and using the FDIC BankFind tool.

No matter where you house your emergency savings fund, it needs to be liquid, meaning you should be able to quickly convert your emergency savings fund to usable cash without withdrawal penalties, whether via debit card, writing a check, or pulling money out of a safe. Most financial professionals don't recommend investing your emergency savings fund in the stock market since stocks are not liquid. To access the funds you have invested in the stock market, you would first need to sell them. After selling, it takes several days for the funds associated with the stock you've sold to be made available to you.

Bonds and certificates of deposit are low-risk options one might use to store their emergency savings fund, but they aren't one hundred percent ideal. Bonds must be sold before you can use them, and there is a cash settlement period involved that can take a few days. Certificates of deposit are a bit more liquid than bonds; however, there are penalties if you withdraw the money early. When it comes to liquidity, the ideal vehicle to store your emergency savings fund is with a savings account or money market account.

Let's not forget accessibility. You should be able to easily access your funds if an emergency occurs. Do not store your emergency savings fund in a bank or credit union across state lines that you don't have a debit card or check-writing privileges for. The same goes for online banks.

What Is a Sinking Fund?

Sinking funds allow you to save a little every month to pay for large, planned expenses. If you review your spending, you'll notice you have expenses that may not occur every month, but they come up every year or season. Examples of these expenses are back-to-school shopping, car repairs, home maintenance, Christmas shopping, vacations, birthday gifts, etc. These expenses typically get put on the back burner and become "emergencies" due to a failure to plan. When they become emergencies, you tend to dip into your emergency savings fund or pull out credit cards to cover them. Sinking funds prevent this. Below is a list of the most common sinking fund categories:

- Car repairs
- Car insurance
- Down payments (car or home)
- Life insurance
- Taxes
- Dental work
- Medication
- Vacation
- Christmas shopping
- Holidays
- Gifts
- School and education fees
- Pets
- Home maintenance and repairs
- Travel

How Do Sinking Funds Work?

With sinking funds, you strategically plan for upcoming expenses by saving a little at a time across multiple categories each month. Now, you may be wondering, *Why can't I just use a regular savings account and save a lump sum of money in it each month?* Truthfully, you can do this, but you'd be missing out on the power of sinking funds. Let's say you have a savings account and contribute $500 to it every month. At the end of twelve months, you decide it's time for a well-deserved trip to Disneyland and use the $6,000 you've saved for your family's tickets, lodging, and accommodations.

Congratulations to you for saving this much, and kudos to you for being able to take your family on a trip they'll remember forever! But what will you do when your laptop that's on its last leg dies and you need a new one? What will you do when that elective medical procedure you've been putting off can't be put off any longer? What do you have planned when the holidays roll around and you want to buy gifts for your friends and family members? This is where most people tap into their emergency savings fund or turn to credit cards for expenses sinking funds could have prevented. Let's look at the example below, where we have $500 per month allocated to four different sinking fund categories:

- $300 for family vacation
- $100 for a new laptop
- $50 for medical expenses
- $50 for holiday shopping

After the span of twelve months, your sinking funds will total:

- $3,600 for a family vacation
- $1,200 for a new laptop
- $600 for medical expenses
- $600 for holiday shopping

With sinking funds, you're still saving $500 each month, but you are spreading it across different categories based on expenses you foresee yourself having during the year. In addition to going on a much-needed family vacation, you know you're going to need a new laptop, and you know you're going to have to schedule and pay for that medical procedure. You know the holidays are going to roll around, and you'll need to buy gifts for your family and friends. So, blindly saving $6,000 and spending it all on a family vacation to Disneyland will leave you feeling trapped and stressed when the other expenses roll around. Sinking funds apply strategy, which changes everything!

How Do an Emergency Savings Fund and a Sinking Fund Differ?

There is a big difference between an emergency savings fund and a sinking fund. An emergency savings fund is money set aside for unexpected expenses during a moment of job loss or catastrophe. You want to do all you can to not dip into your emergency savings fund, and if you're lucky, you might go years without having to use it. On the other hand, a sinking fund is money reserved to be spent soon. As you progress through your wealth and budgeting journey, you'll find expenses that were previously emergencies are now expenses you are able to forecast and include in your sinking funds.

Why Are Sinking Funds Important?

Sinking funds are vital to one's wealth strategy for a myriad of reasons. First and foremost, sinking funds empower you to be prepared for expected yet unwanted expenses. The reality is a lot of expenses are financially unexpected, but they are mentally expected. Having a sinking fund for expenses you pray won't come up but kind of know will, such as taxes, the copay for your annual physical, or your yearly car tune-up, will make these expenses less painful when the time comes.

Secondly, sinking funds give you the ability to tell your money what to do versus being limited to the money you have on hand. Let's say you want to take a trip to Asia, but you're strapped for cash. Regardless of your current financial situation, you can still go on this trip by creating a sinking fund. Research the total cost for the trip, set a realistic deadline, and save small amounts toward this getaway each month.

Thirdly, sinking funds allow you to "treat yourself" with none of the guilt that usually comes with doing so. Using your disposable income to treat yourself regularly can wreak havoc on your finances, but through the use of sinking funds, you can identify a few luxuries you want to indulge in and save for them every month.

And finally, sinking funds prevent you from dipping into your emergency savings fund or, worse, incurring debt. Guess what! Those unwanted expenses I referenced earlier are going to come up. If you don't have sinking funds set up for them, you're going to have to dip into your emergency savings fund when they occur. If you don't have an emergency savings fund or if you don't have enough money in the fund to cover the expense, you're going to reach for a credit card.

Where Should I Store My Sinking Funds?

Your sinking funds can be stored in any type of savings account. You can even store them in a certificate of deposit, a money market account, or a high-yield savings account to take advantage of the higher interest rates. Unlike an emergency savings fund, which you would need to access immediately in an emergency, you have leeway with where you store your sinking funds since you have an idea of when you will be dipping into them. When it comes to the logistics of managing your sinking funds, you have a few options:

- You can store your sinking funds as one lump sum amount and manually track how much money is allocated to each category.
- You can open up a savings account for each sinking fund category.
- You can allocate an envelope to each fund category and add cash to the envelopes as you see fit.

What Is a Cash Cushion?

Traditionally, a cash cushion is an account with a balance of a few hundred dollars to avoid overdrafts. This account is typically linked to one's primary checking account. Although having a cash cushion to prevent overdrafts is a great idea, it's best to expand its usage for months where small expenses pile up or months where you don't do a great job sticking to your budget. It's nice to have $200 to $300 on reserve at all times for these months. Let's face it: You're not going to stick to your budget every month, so why not be prepared? The wealth journey spans an entire lifetime, and during your life, you're going to have months where you fall off the wagon.

Some have a few hundred in their cash cushion, and others like to have at least $1,000. The great thing about cash cushions is they are low-balance accounts, so they are easy to get started and less intimidating than an emergency savings fund or sinking fund; you could literally set a goal of having a cash cushion of $250.

Conclusion

In this chapter, we covered the various accounts one should have as buffers to prevent them from establishing more credit card debt, borrowing from their 401(k), or turning to high-interest loans. This chapter may have been very intimidating for you. After all, saving money is hard. This chapter's purpose wasn't to overwhelm or frustrate you but, rather, introduce you to emergency savings funds, sinking funds, cash cushions, and their uses and associated benefits.

I would love for you to finish reading this chapter and promptly have an emergency savings fund with a $30,000 balance, various sinking funds, and a hefty cash cushion, but that would be incredibly unrealistic. It took me several years of hard work before I built up my emergency savings fund to an amount I was proud of, established sinking funds that were replenished continuously, and maintained a healthy cash cushion.

After reading this chapter, you should be mulling over how much money you would need to have set aside in case of an emergency, exploring the various exciting sinking funds you want to set up, and toying around with the idea of a cash cushion.

Activity

As discussed in this chapter, sinking funds allow you to plan for large expenses by breaking them into monthly, bite-sized, manageable chunks. For this chapter's activity, you can get started with sinking funds by creating a list of expenses you foresee occurring in the coming year and calculating how much you need to contribute to these funds each month. Car repairs, a down payment for a new car, vacation(s), holiday shopping, gifts, and travel are a few examples to get your wheels turning. On a sheet of paper, write down four columns: Sinking Fund, Total Cost, Payment Period, and Monthly Cost.

1. Narrow your list down to three expenses you want to create a sinking fund for, and write them down in the "Sinking Fund" column.
2. Figure out the total cost for each planned expense and write the numbers in the "Total Cost" column.
3. In the "Payment Period" column, write down the number of months you have before these expenses come up.
4. The "Monthly Cost" column requires calculation. Divide the amount you wrote in the "Total Cost" column by the number of months you've forecasted in the "Payment Period" column. The number from this calculation will give you the "Monthly Cost" for each planned expense. This is the amount you should be setting aside each month in anticipation of these expenses.

RULE #5

Optimize Your Debt-to-Income Ratio by Aggressively Paying off Debt

I went through a period in my early twenties when I didn't answer calls from unknown or 800 numbers because 99.9 percent of the time, they were from debt collectors. In between dodging debt collector calls and failing miserably at adjusting to life post-college, I had developed a special ritual. Every time I checked my mail, I would separate my real mail from my junk mail and the mail from my debt collectors. I would take the letters from my debt collectors and stash them in the bottom drawer of my IKEA dresser. My reasoning was "out of sight, out of mind."

This strategy worked for a while. Mentally, I was at peace with my debt. The debt collection calls were at a minimum, as I had done an exemplary job of blocking them. And as for the debt collection letters? My IKEA dresser's drawer became stuffed with collection notices until the bottom began to sag. But eventually, reality set in. Like most twenty-somethings fresh out of college, I was at an age where I needed to make big purchases. I had just moved to Miami from New York and needed to 1) purchase a car and 2) rent an apartment, both of which required credit checks. Unfortunately, my daily rituals of blocking debt collector calls and hiding collection letters had my credit score in the gutter.

The story ends with me getting the apartment and purchasing the car but with strings attached. Thanks to my terrible credit, I had to pay close to three months' rent and a security deposit for the apartment. For the car, I had to borrow money from my mom for the down payment and drove off the lot in a hooptie since my credit severely limited the amount of money banks were willing to loan me. It was a much-needed lesson. After I was settled into my new apartment and had made peace with the car, I blocked off a weekend where I went through my drawer of collection notices and set up payment arrangements with each and every creditor.

Negative Consequences of Debt

Being in debt affects your life in more ways than you can imagine. Being trapped in debt can tie up your money to the point where you can't do what you want with it. What's worse, the effects of debt are far more than just financial. On a day-to-day basis, relentless calls and letters from creditors can make your life miserable. The stress of dealing with debt can have a destructive effect on your personal relationships and even your health. In the following sections, we will detail some of the significant consequences associated with debt.

Consequence #1: Negative Impact on Credit Score

The primary consequence of debt is the negative impact it has on your credit score. A credit score is a rating assigned to individuals that indicates to lenders their capacity to repay a loan; it proves the creditworthiness of an individual. Credit scores range from 350 to 850. The higher your credit score, the lower the risk associated with lending to you. The five components that make up your credit score are as follows:

- Payment history
- Amounts owed
- Length of credit history
- Credit mix
- New credit

Out of these five components, payment history and amounts owed account for sixty-five percent of your credit score. These two categories are directly tied to your debt. Payment history is the record you've established by either paying on time or not paying the bills associated with your debt. A positive payment history indicates you've paid all your loans, credit cards, etc., on time and as agreed. An adverse payment history reflects that you've missed payments and/or had late payments.

Amounts owed indicates you have credit balances owed. This isn't necessarily a bad thing; however, if you have two credit cards, one with a $6,000 credit limit and the other with a $5,000 credit limit and you've maxed out both, this indicates you are carrying a lot of debt, and a considerable amount of your income may be going toward debt payments.

When creditors pull your credit report and find it riddled with late or missed payments and/or maxed-out credit cards, this indicates you are a risky person to loan money; not to mention, these patterns are typically associated with a low credit score.

Consequence #2: Wage Garnishment

Not being in control of your debt can lead to wage garnishment, which is more common than people think. Wage garnishment occurs when you haven't made a payment toward a debt and the creditor gets a court order to get your employer to divert up to twenty-five percent of your disposable income toward the debt. Wage garnishment typically occurs until the debt is paid off.

Once your wages begin to get garnished, it is difficult, if not impossible, to get the garnishments to stop. This unfortunate situation causes embarrassment for the employee and additional paperwork for the employer. You cannot be fired because of a wage garnishment; however, this legal protection is only in place if you have one wage garnishment proceeding. If your wages are being garnished for two or more debts, this protection no longer exists, and you are no longer shielded from retaliation.

Consequence #3: Bank Garnishment

A bank account garnishment means a debt collector is legally allowed to remove money from your bank account to repay an outstanding debt. This is usually a last resort creditors use when debtors ignore requests to pay back what they owe. With wage garnishment, a collector can't take more than twenty-five percent of a debtor's paycheck; however, if that paycheck is deposited in a bank and the creditor gets a bank garnishment against you, all the money in the account can be grabbed to pay down the debt. The creditor can only take up to the amount you owe, but if you owe $12,000 and have $6,000 in the bank, they can legally take every penny of it.

Bank garnishments disrupt one's life, as your bank will typically freeze your account during this period to prevent you from withdrawing money from the account until the garnishment has taken place. This might cause you to miss your rent or mortgage payments. Bank garnishments have pushed many into bankruptcy, foreclosure, and even eviction.

Consequence #4: Tax Refund Garnishment

Many aren't aware of this, but the U.S Treasury Department's Bureau of the Fiscal Service is the same agency that issues tax refunds. This agency has the authority to hold all or part of your return to cover certain debts you owe. While your tax refund can't be intercepted for a defaulted mortgage, car loan, or credit card, it can be intercepted for the following:

- **Child Support:** If you are behind on your child support payments, your state's child support agency can request that the Treasury Department withhold all or part of your federal tax refund to cover back payments.
- **Student Loans:** If you have student loans that are federally insured and you default on them, the federal government can garnish your federal income tax to help repay them.
- **State Unemployment Compensation:** If you collected more unemployment benefits than you were entitled,

whether by accident or due to fraud, your federal tax return can be garnished to repay this obligation.

- **State Income Taxes:** Your federal income tax return can be intercepted to cover unpaid state income taxes.
- **Federal Income Taxes:** If you owe federal income taxes, your refund can be taken to pay them.
- **Spousal Support:** An award for spousal support that's associated with a child support order can result in your tax refund being garnished if payments are overdue.

Consequence #5: Negative Impact on Career

Employers in certain industries now include credit reports in their background checks. Many employers believe financially responsible employees are better workers, and those struggling financially may be distracted and tempted to steal. A credit report with late payments may indicate that a candidate isn't organized or responsible. Mishandling your personal finances might give an employer pause when it comes to hiring you, especially if your role involves handling company money or making financial decisions. Adverse credit reports don't just affect job hunters; some companies even run credit checks before offering an employee a promotion.

Consequence #6: Bankruptcy

For those drowning in debt, with collapsed finances that have made them unable to make any movement toward conquering them, bankruptcy may offer a legal lifeline. Essentially, going bankrupt is when a consumer petitions the court to release them from the liability of their debts. Sounds too good to be true? It is. Bankruptcy stops collection agency calls and garnishments and erases most debt, but it comes with negative consequences. Bankruptcy lingers on your credit report for seven to ten years after filing and reduces your ability to obtain new credit and financing for several years. Depending on where you are in life, bankruptcy can severely cripple you.

Benefits of Being Debt-Free

The benefits of living debt-free are often life changing. Unshackling yourself from debt frees up cash, which means you get to keep more of your take-home pay. In a lot of cases, this means breaking the cycle of living paycheck to paycheck. Instead of being beholden to creditors, you can use the money you were previously putting toward your debt to further your other financial goals, such as building up your emergency savings fund, investing, or beefing up your retirement contributions. Let's not forget the instant boost of one's credit score that comes from managing your debt.

Being debt-free is also good for your health. The link between mental illnesses and financial stress has been proven time and time again. Being debt-free literally lifts a financial and emotional weight off your shoulders. In the following sections, we will detail some of the benefits of being debt-free.

Benefit #1: Frees Up Cash Flow

One of the most significant benefits of being debt-free is that it frees up your cash flow and has a positive effect on your debt-to-income ratio. When you have debt, a large portion of your income is tied to debt payments. Let's say you purchase a $25,000 car with a 4.21% interest rate on a six-year term. All things considered, you'd be looking at payments of around $394 each month.

That $394 could be used on other wealth-building initiatives, such as contributions toward your children's college funds, savings, starting a business, investing, or even charitable giving. If you were to pay off the car early, that would be $394 in income you'd be able to keep versus having to allocate it toward debt. Annually, that's close to $5,000 in income you'd be retaining.

Benefit #2: Reduces Stress

Another benefit of being debt-free or even getting marginally better at managing your debt is stress reduction. Imagine the mental clarity you'd possess because you don't have to dodge letters or phone calls from debt collectors. Some people have gotten physically sick from the stress associated with debt. Their finances have encumbered them to the point where they are constantly worrying and experiencing side effects, such as heartburn, stomach knots, migraines, anxiety, depression, and panic attacks. To make matters worse, social stigmas and shame are associated with debt, so people tend to keep these issues bottled up instead of talking about their debt and related emotions with family and close friends.

Benefit #3: Better Credit Score

Credit utilization is the amount of debt you're carrying compared to the amount of credit you have. Credit utilization accounts for thirty percent of one's credit score. Paying down your debt so your credit utilization is lowered jump-starts your financial journey in a positive direction.

How to Conquer Debt

In this chapter, we've discussed the paralyzing effects debt can have on your life and the beauty of being debt-free. Now, you're probably wondering, *How do I go about living this dream life where all my debt is paid off, my credit score is in the 700s, I'm not living paycheck to paycheck, and I can spend my money as I please?* There's no easy way out of this one. To make this lifestyle your reality, you'll need to conquer your debt. In the next few sections, we'll get down to the nitty-gritty and review tried and true methods for tackling debt: the debt avalanche and debt snowball methods. Both of these methods have been used by thousands of people, including myself, to conquer their debt.

Method 1: Debt Avalanche Method

The debt avalanche method targets debt with the highest interest rate first. This route helps you save time and interest over your debt payoff journey. With the debt avalanche method, you make minimum payments on all your debts; however, any additional funds you have go toward the debt with the highest interest.

If you have a medical bill that is $600 with no interest, a Macy's credit card with a balance of $5,000 and a 25% interest rate, and a Capital One credit card with a $1,000 balance and a 15.9% interest rate, you would make minimum payments on all debts but prioritize the Macy's credit card, followed by the Capital One credit card, and finally, the medical bill.

DEBT	BALANCE	INTEREST RATE	MINIMUM PAYMENT
Macy's Credit Card	$5,000	25%	$100
Capital One Credit Card	$1,000	15.9%	$150
Medical Bill	$600	0%	$50

Once the debt with the highest interest rate is entirely paid, you can apply the minimum payment, as well as additional payments you were making, toward the debt with the next highest interest rate on your list. Let's say the minimum payment amounts required for each of these debts totals $300 each month. Besides these minimum payments, you would need to decide how much extra beyond that $300 you can allocate each month to tackle your debt.

Let's say you have an extra $200 a month to contribute toward your debt outside of the $300 minimum payments. You'll make the monthly minimum payment on each debt and allocate the extra $200 to your Macy's credit card since it has the highest interest rate. That would have you paying $300 a month on your Macy's credit card until it is paid off.

Once that's paid, you can move on to your Capital One credit card. You'll make minimum payments on all debts, but take the former minimum amount you were paying toward your Macy's credit card, as well as the extra $200 you've allocated toward your debt payoff, and reallocate it to your Capital One credit card. This will have you paying $450 on the Capital One credit card until it is paid off.

You would then pivot to your medical bill. You'll pay the minimum payment of fifty dollars and take the former minimum payments of your Macy's and Capital One credit cards and the $200 you've set aside for paying off debt and apply them to your medical bill. This comes out to $500 a month going toward your medical bill until it is paid off.

Method 2: Debt Snowball Method

With the debt snowball method, your debt is paid off in order from smallest to largest balance, no matter the interest rate. When your smallest debt is paid, you roll the amount you put toward that debt into the next smallest debt on your list. The debt snowball method utilizes the power of motivation, as the small wins associated with this method are believed to keep you motivated to stay on track.

Let's say you have a medical bill that is $600 with no interest, a Macy's credit card with a balance of $5,000 and a 25% interest rate, and a Capital One credit card with a $1,000 balance and a 15.9% interest rate. Using the debt snowball method, you would prioritize your medical bill, followed by your Capital One credit card, and finally, your Macy's credit card.

DEBT	BALANCE	INTEREST RATE	MINIMUM PAYMENT
Medical Bill	$600	0%	$50
Capital One Credit Card	$1,000	15.9%	$150
Macy's Credit Card	$5,000	25%	$100

You'll make the monthly minimum payments on all debt, which would total $300 monthly. Outside of these minimum payments, you would need to decide how much extra beyond that $300 you can allocate each month to paying off your debt. Let's say you have an extra $200 a month you're able to contribute toward your debt payments outside of the $300 minimum payments. You'll make the monthly minimum payments on each debt and allocate the extra $200 to your medical bill since it has the lowest balance. You'll be spending $250 a month on the medical bill until it is paid off.

Once that's paid, you would move on to your Capital One credit card. You'll make minimum payments on all debts, but take the former minimum payment you were paying toward your medical bill, as well as the extra $200 you've allocated toward debt, and reallocate it toward your Capital One credit card. This will have you paying $400 on the Capital One credit card until it's paid off.

You would then pivot to your Macy's credit card. You'd make the minimum payment of one hundred dollars toward this credit card, plus the minimum payments that were being contributed to your medical bill and Capital One credit card. You would also contribute the $200 you've set aside for debt payments toward this card. This comes out to $500 a month toward your Macy's credit card until it is paid off.

Debt Snowball vs. Debt Avalanche

Deciding between the debt snowball and debt avalanche method boils down to your resolve and consistency. The debt avalanche method is faster and cheaper, as you minimize the interest incurred; however, it can be daunting. Depending on the size of your debts and their associated interest rates, it can be a while before your first debt is paid off. This might lead to discouragement, which could cause you to fall off the wagon. You might feel like you aren't getting anywhere with your debt payoff journey and go back to only making the minimum payments, late payments, or worse, completely missing payments.

If you decide to go with the debt snowball method, you might pay more over time than you would with the debt avalanche method. This method doesn't take interest rates into account, so you might end up paying off your higher-interest debt later. Putting off paying your higher-interest debt will cost you more in interest fees.

It boils down to this: If you need short-term victories to inspire you, your best bet will be to use the debt snowball method. If you are analytical and patient, the debt avalanche method may appeal to you.

Other Helpful Tips for Conquering Debt

In addition to implementing either the debt snowball or debt avalanche method to tackle your debt, in the next few sections, I'll be sharing some foolproof tips that, when executed, will guarantee your debt is paid off ASAP.

Tip # 1: Pay More Than the Minimum Balance

Making only minimum payments on a credit card will keep the card in good standing; however, it has terrible repercussions. If you only make the minimum payment, you will pay more in interest, and it will take you longer to pay off the balance.

Let's say you have a credit card with a $7,000 balance and a

15.9% interest rate, with a minimum payment requirement of $200. Making only the minimum payment would add thousands of dollars to your total credit card bill.

	FORECAST BASED ON MINIMUM $200 PAYMENT	FORECAST BASED ON ADDITIONAL PAYMENT OF $100
CREDIT CARD BALANCE	$7,000	$7,000
INTEREST RATE	15.9%	15.9%
PAYMENT PER MONTH	$200	$300
PAYOFF TIME	48 Months	29 Months
INTEREST PAID	$2,469	$1,430

A $200 monthly minimum payment, for instance, would take an estimated four years to pay off completely (roughly forty-eight months), and you'd wind up paying an additional $2,469 in interest on the $7,000 balance. However, if you were to pay the minimum balance of $200 plus an extra one hundred dollars, it would take an estimated two-and-a-half years to pay it off completely (roughly twenty-nine months), and you'd only pay $1,430 in interest on the $7,000 balance.

Tip #2: Put Work Bonuses, Tax Refunds, and Commissions Toward the Debt

Chipping away at your debt every month can be a long and draining process. To speed up your debt repayment, I recommend putting your work bonuses, tax refunds, and any other money you might stumble upon toward your debt. If you're able to make a large payment of $2,500 on a credit card with a balance of $5,000, thanks to a tax refund or work bonus, this will lower the amount of time it will take you to pay off the debt. Additionally, this will reduce the amount of interest you have to pay on the debt in the long run.

Tip #3: Realize There's No Easy Way Out

Some people have a hard time managing their debt by themselves and turn to the assistance of credit repair companies. Be cautious when taking this route and be sure to do your research. There are several shady credit repair companies that target financially distressed people riddled with credit problems and insurmountable debt. These fraudulent companies lure clients by promising to remove negative information from their credit reports, even if it's correct. They falsely promise to negotiate with creditors to settle or reduce their client's repayment obligations, charging them substantial fees up front but failing to help them actually settle or lower their debts.

If you struggle with managing your debt yourself, there are non-profit agencies that can provide credit repair services at a minimal cost. If you're going through financial hardship, you can even get the costs waived in some instances. But remember, there is no easy way to be debt-free, and legitimate agencies require work on your end. The primary service these non-profit agencies offer is education, which includes instructing consumers on the different components of a credit score, the basics of budgeting, and money management. You will work with them to get to the bottom of your spending habits, create a budget, and set up a plan for debt repayment.

Conclusion

Debt is overwhelming, especially when it is stretched across multiple credit cards and account types and is assigned to various collection agencies. Debt can be an albatross that affects everything from your finances to your emotional and physical health. Tackling debt isn't easy nor fun. It is a daunting journey that requires discipline and perseverance. It only takes a few missed bills and splurges to become riddled with debt, while it takes years to get out of it. When you're swimming in red-letter bills and harassing phone calls from debt collection agencies, it can often feel like there's no way out, but by using tried and trusted strategies, such as the debt avalanche and debt snowball methods, you can eventually free yourself from the shackles of debt.

During this journey, life events will undoubtedly come up. You will need to pay off debt while paying for a wedding, facing a death in the family, moving to a new city, going through a career change, getting a divorce, having a baby, etc. Let's also not forget that the debt-free journey isn't just about paying off old debt, but about correcting and getting to the root of previous behaviors to prevent new debt from being established. The only way to stay on course is by being disciplined with both your debt payments and your spending behavior. Every day, you will be triggered. It's going to be up to you and the boundaries you have set with your money to navigate these triggers and turn them from hurdles into stepping stones.

Activity

It is human nature to shy away from uncomfortable situations, but doing so is the antithesis of this book. For this chapter's activity, you're going to face your discomfort head-on by checking and examining your credit report.

Step 1: Access your credit report.

You're entitled to one free copy of your credit report every twelve months from each of the three national credit reporting bureaus: Experian, Equifax, and TransUnion. To access your free copies, go to AnnualCreditReport.com and provide the following information to verify your identity:

- Legal name
- Social Security number
- Date of birth
- Current address
- Previous address (if you've lived at your current address for less than two years)

You can obtain all three of your credit reports at one time or request them over time. Once you've gained access to your reports, you can begin reviewing them. Experian, TransUnion, and Equifax credit reports are all formatted differently; however, they all contain the same general types of information.

Step 2: Review your personal information.

First, you want to make sure all your personal information is correct. Your personal information is used as a means for creditors to identify you and has no bearing on your actual credit score. However, inconsistencies in this section can hint to whether you've been a victim of identity theft or credit card fraud. The most common errors found when reviewing this section of your credit report are as follows:

- Your personal information being meshed with someone who has a similar name
- Information, such as name, address, or phone number, showing as inaccurate or incomplete
- No prior address listed if you have not lived long enough at your current address
- Inaccurate Social Security number or date of birth
- Outdated, missing, or incorrect employment information

Step 3: Review your credit accounts.

Your report will list each of your credit accounts and their details. For each account, you'll have a summary section that shows the following details:

- Lender
- Account number

- Available credit
- Reported balance
- Debt-to-credit ratio

For each account, you will also have an account details section that shows the following details:

- Account type (revolving, installment, open)
- Credit limit
- Highest balance reported on the account
- Minimum monthly payment
- Loan type (mortgage, education loan, auto loan, credit card, etc.)
- Date opened
- Date closed
- Last payment date
- Amount past due
- Your responsibility for the account (individual, cosigner, joint, authorized user, etc.)
- Payment history
- Current status (open, closed, late, paid as agreed, charged off, etc.)

The following are details to look for when reviewing accounts on your credit report:

- Accounts you did not cosign for mistakenly listing you as a cosigner
- Closed accounts inaccurately listed as open
- Accounts you are an authorized user of not being included in the report

- Accounts you closed not being indicated as "closed by consumer" (if not, it looks like the creditor or lender closed the accounts)
- A delinquent account from over seven years ago or a delinquent account that does not include the date of the delinquency
- A discharged debt still showing as owed
- An account opened as a result of identity theft
- Debts your spouse incurred before marriage being attributed to you
- Accounts commingled with someone with a similar name
- An account only your spouse is responsible for being listed as joint
- Incorrect account histories, such as late payments, being noted when you've paid on time
- Accounts with credit limits and loan balances that are incorrect

While reviewing this section, you may be surprised to find closed accounts on your report. Remember, a credit report shows a history of your credit accounts. This history includes both open and closed accounts, but there are some time limitations. Closed accounts with negative remarks remain on your report for up to seven years. Closed accounts with positive remarks remain for up to ten years.

STEP 4: REVIEW YOUR NEGATIVE PUBLIC RECORDS.

This section of your credit report will display negative public financial records associated with your debts. In the past, this section included bankruptcies, judgments, and tax liens; however, in 2017, the three nationwide credit reporting companies, Equifax, Experian, and TransUnion, entered into a settlement called the National Consumer Assistance Plan (NCAP).[6] One of the conditions of this settlement is public records must meet strict requirements to appear on consumer credit reports. Civil judgments and tax liens were found to not meet the new strict requirements and, thus, were removed from all credit reports.

Presently, the only derogatory public record that should appear on your credit report is bankruptcy. If you find a tax lien or civil judgment while reviewing your credit reports, you should immediately dispute that record with the credit reporting agencies.

By law, public bankruptcy records remain on your credit report for the following periods:

- Chapter 7 bankruptcy remains on your credit report for ten years after the filing date.
- Chapter 13 bankruptcy typically remains on your credit report for seven years after the filing date; however, in some cases, it can remain for up to ten years.

Details to look for when reviewing negative public records on your credit report are as follows:

- Bankruptcies filed by a spouse or ex-spouse
- Bankruptcies not identified by the specific chapter of the bankruptcy code
- Chapter 7 bankruptcy filed over ten years ago
- Chapter 13 filed over seven years ago

- Tax liens
- Judgments

Step 5: Review your credit inquiries.

A credit inquiry occurs when a lender or creditor pulls your credit record. Your credit report will have a section that lists all inquiries made on your credit history. Each inquiry will list the date the inquiry occurred, the company who made the inquiry, and a description of why the inquiry was requested (account review inquiry, promotional inquiry, prequalification for installment, etc.)

There are two varieties of credit inquiries: hard inquiries and soft inquiries. Hard inquiries are the result of lenders checking your credit for the sake of making a lending decision. Hard inquiries show you applied to get credit somewhere, whether it was a car loan, mortgage, student loan, or credit card. Unfortunately, hard inquiries decrease your credit score by five to ten points on average. Depending on the state your credit score was in before the inquiry, these points can mean the difference between fair credit and poor credit.

Keeping this in mind, be mindful of the credit you apply for and how often you apply. The following applications can lead to hard inquiries:

- Mortgage
- Credit card
- Student loan
- Auto loan
- Personal loan
- Apartment rental

Hard inquiries affect your credit score for a year and stay on your credit report for twenty-four months. The other type of credit inquiry is known as a soft inquiry. A soft inquiry may occur when you check your own credit or when a credit card issuer checks your credit without your permission to preapprove you for a credit card offer sent to you via the mail. Your employer might also run a soft inquiry before hiring you or offering you a promotion. Soft inquiries don't affect your credit scores. The following can lead to soft inquiries:

- Checking your credit score
- "Pre-qualified" credit card offers
- "Pre-qualified" insurance quotes
- Employment verification
- Background checks

While reviewing the inquiry section of your credit report, keep in mind the information presented in this section is specific to the credit reporting agency that produced the report. For example, if you're looking at a TransUnion report, you will see lenders who conducted a credit inquiry on your TransUnion credit report. The same goes for Equifax and Experian.

Step 6: Review consumer statements.

Under the Fair Credit Reporting Act, you are allowed to add a one-hundred-word "Consumer Statement" to your credit reports. The Consumer Statement section is a space in your credit report for you to challenge or explain, in one hundred words or less, any credit entry in your credit report file. You can also use this section to dispute or explain your credit report in its entirety, with the stipulation that you use no more than one hundred words.

There are two types of consumer statements you can have added to your credit report. The first is an account-specific statement, and the second is a general statement. An account-specific statement is linked to a specific account in your credit report. For example, if you were unable to make payments on your car loan due to extenuating circumstances, such as extended unemployment or medical illness, you can add an account-specific statement explaining this circumstance.

The other type of consumer statement is a general statement. A general statement is linked to multiple accounts on your credit report or your credit report in its entirety. A general statement can be used to explain your overall credit situation. An example of a scenario where you would use a general statement is if you went through a period of financial hardship, which resulted in missed/late payments across multiple accounts.

When it comes to utilizing consumer statements, be cautious. Account-specific statements fall off your credit report when the account is deleted, but general statements stay on your report for two years. In two years, you might be able to drastically increase your credit score, but you'll be stuck with a one-hundred-word statement that alludes to payment and credit issues you've had in the past that are no longer relevant.

STEP 7: REVIEW FRAUD ALERTS.

A fraud alert is a notice placed on your credit report informing creditors and lenders that you may have been a victim of fraud or identity theft.[7] A fraud alert warns creditors to take additional steps in verifying your identity before extending you credit.

Fraud alerts make it difficult for an identity thief to open accounts in your name. According to the Federal Trade Commission, a few reasons you might reach out to a credit bureau to have a fraud alert placed on your credit report are as follows:[8]

- Someone has misused your personal information.
- You're concerned about identity theft but haven't yet become a victim.
- Your wallet, Social Security card, or other personal, financial, or account information is lost or stolen.
- Your personal information was exposed in a data breach.

Fraud alerts are free, and the initial credit bureau you contact must tell the other two about your alert. For example, if you reach out to Experian to have a fraud alert added, Experian must notify TransUnion and Equifax about this alert so they can add it to their versions of your credit report. When it comes to fraud alerts, you have three options: an initial fraud alert, an extended fraud alert, and an active duty fraud alert. With all of these alerts, companies are encouraged to take reasonable steps to verify your identity before extending you credit.

The first type of alert, an initial fraud alert, is the easiest to add, and it's a sensible precaution, even if you only suspect fraud has occurred. An initial fraud alert lasts one year, and you do not have to prove you've been a victim of fraud to add this alert.

The second type of alert is an extended fraud alert. With this type of fraud alert, you have to provide proof you've been a victim of identity theft by completing and submitting an identity theft report that includes a copy of a police report. The extended fraud alert stays on your credit reports for seven years.

The third type of alert is an active duty fraud alert. Those on active duty can place an active duty alert on their credit reports to minimize their risk of becoming victims of identity theft while deployed. Active duty alerts last for one year.

STEP 8: SUBMIT DISPUTES.

Throughout this activity, you've been asked to review various sections of your credit report. If you found inaccurate, fraudulent, or missing information while reviewing your credit report, you'll need to dispute these discrepancies with the credit bureau that produced the report. For example, if you found an error while reviewing your Experian report, you would send in a dispute to Experian. In the following sections, we'll cover some of the common pitfalls people face when disputing items on their credit reports.

Pitfall #1: Disputing Accurate Information

Accurate information cannot be removed from your credit report; however, under the Fair Credit Reporting Act, all credit bureaus are liable if they fail to observe your debt's time limit. If you see a valid debt on your credit report that is past its time limit, you can dispute it and demand its removal. By law, negative credit information, including delinquent and charged-off loans or accounts, can remain on your credit reports for up to seven years. Bankruptcies remain on your report for up to ten years.

Pitfall #2: Lost Evidence or Lack of Documentation

You can't simply tell a credit reporting bureau that your credit report's information is incorrect and expect them to fix it. You have to provide evidence to back the dispute. Let's say you have a credit card on your credit report that incorrectly shows a history of late payments. Proving that the history of late payments is inaccurate may look like providing a copy of cleared checks or even presenting copies of bank statements that verify you've, in fact, made payments on time.

If you have repeatedly filed the same dispute and it has gotten nowhere, the next step would be to escalate the dispute to the Consumer Financial Protection Bureau, the Federal Trade Commission, or your local Attorney General's office. To successfully escalate your dispute in addition to proving the negative entry on your credit report is false, you will need to do the following:

- Show that you've made legitimate attempts to get the negative information corrected
- Show that you've been substantially harmed by the credit bureau failing to rectify the issue

Again, documentation and evidence will be needed. Establishing that you've made legitimate attempts to get the erroneous information removed from your credit report may look like providing a certified mail receipt from when you mailed your dispute to the credit bureau. Showing you've been substantially harmed by the credit bureau failing to correct the information may look like getting documentation when a lender informs you that the negative entry on your credit report has caused you to be rejected for a loan.

Pitfall #3: Dealing Only with the Lender

Many reach out to the lender or furnisher of an account directly when they see inaccurate information on their credit report. An example of this would be if your old cell phone account is shown as being sent to collections when you know and have evidence you paid your final bill, so you reach out to your old cell phone carrier to get them to fix the issue.

But despite reaching out to the lender, you will still need to file a dispute with the credit bureau where the inaccurate information appears. You can dispute the accuracy of information with your lender or the furnisher of an account, but if they insist the records are correct, you can't sue them, which leaves you with very little recourse if they fail to correct the mistake.

Pitfall #4: Disputing Errors via Online Forms

Credit reporting agencies have made it very convenient to dispute errors online. Unfortunately, these online systems have character limits and do not give you enough room to state your case thoroughly. Using the tiny online forms supplied by the credit bureaus without attaching additional evidence or a longer letter detailing your dispute doesn't give you enough room to make a full explanation. To ensure your dispute has a fighting chance, type and mail it, as well as your supporting evidence, to the credit bureau via certified mail.

Pitfall #5: Thinking They're Done Once They've Submitted Disputes

After receiving your disputes, the credit bureaus will reach out to the lender or furnisher of the account that provided the information you're disputing. The lender or furnisher of the account has thirty to forty-five days to respond. When the credit bureau receives a response, they will notify you of the outcome of the investigation.

If the credit bureau does not receive a response, they will correct or delete the information as you've requested. However, in many instances, the account's lender or furnisher responds, and your dispute is denied. Upon receiving a denial, you will need to send in additional supporting documents or evidence to prove your case.

RULE #6

Prepare for Your Future by Contributing to Your 401(k)

My first post-undergrad job was for a start-up located in the heart of Manhattan. For a girl who who grew up in the middle of nowhere, it was a dream come true. The company had an open floor plan, a Ping-Pong table smack dab in the middle of the dining area, and a dress code so relaxed, it became uncomfortable (the CEO wore an Adidas tracksuit to work every day). It was the quintessential start-up.

As with every start-up, the CEO was big on feedback. During one of our morning huddles, he asked each employee to send him an email detailing a few initiatives we wanted the company to embark upon. The emails we sent in were varied but among the same lines: We wanted more social activities. I specifically requested we increase our happy hours from one to two times per week and put a social committee in place to plan bonding and trust-building activities among employees.

During lunch one muggy summer afternoon, we were

discussing the emails we'd sent in when it became apparent there was a detractor among us. One of our coworkers confessed she'd emailed the CEO requesting he offer 401(k) plans to all employees. We chastised her.

"We're in our early twenties; none of us should be thinking about 401(k) plans right now," I vividly remember someone telling her. I had no idea what a 401(k) was and preferred the idea of more happy hours over this far-fetched concept she was presenting, so I joined in with the teasing. In hindsight, I was the fool.

The backlash against 401(k) plans being offered instead of more social activities was so great, that the CEO went with the latter and treated us to more happy hours, dinners, and team-bonding events. If only the CEO had ignored our youthful ignorance and went with the 401(k) recommendation instead! I would have started contributing to my 401(k) at twenty-two rather than twenty-five and would have several thousand more dollars sitting in my bank account when it came time to retire. Let's just say every time I check my retirement account, I can't help but daydream of what could have been.

What Is a 401(k)?

What exactly is a 401(k), and why was my coworker so adamant about them being offered to employees? A 401(k) is a retirement plan that allows a company's eligible employees to save and invest for retirement. 401(k) plans, which are one of the building blocks of wealth and have transformed the way Americans approach retirement, were created by accident, coming to existence when Congress passed the Revenue Act of 1978. This act included a provision, Section 401(k), that gave employees a way to keep portions of their compensation from being taxed.[9]

In 1980, Ted Benna, a benefits consultant who, at the time, was tasked with helping one of his bank clients create a more tax-friendly retirement program, came up with the idea of using Section 401(k) to allow employees to defer pre-tax money into a retirement plan while receiving an employer match.[10] But therein lay a problem: The original 401(k) provision did not allow for this type of account to be set up and funded through salary reductions. Benna didn't let this dissuade him. He petitioned the IRS to modify Section 401(k) of the Revenue Act of 1978, and in 1981, the IRS complied. A few years later, nearly all major corporations were offering 401(k) plans to their employees.

My coworker wanted 401(k) plans to be offered to us because the earlier you start contributing to a 401(k), the better, thanks to the beauty of compound interest. There are two types of 401(k) plans: traditional and Roth. With a traditional 401(k), your contributions are made pre-tax, and your money grows tax deferred. You're taxed once you retire and begin making withdrawals. With a Roth 401(k), your contributions are made post-tax, which means you will not be taxed when you make withdrawals during retirement.

Making the decision between participating in a traditional or Roth 401(k) is based on two factors. First, does your place of employment even offer a Roth 401(k)? Not all companies do. You may be at a company that only offers a traditional 401(k). Secondly, what tax bracket are you presently in, and what tax bracket do you think you'll be in when it's time to retire? If you're currently in a lower tax bracket but expect to be taxed in a higher bracket when you reach retirement, a Roth 401(k) may be the best option. Or you might be a high-income worker who prefers a traditional 401(k) because you are currently taxed in a higher tax bracket and expect to be in a lower tax bracket when you retire. In some instances, you don't have to pick between the two; some employers allow you to contribute to both.

Why Do You Need a 401(k)?

In a perfect world, three components would work together to ensure one is financially prepared for retirement:

- Social Security benefits
- Pension offered by employer
- Personal retirement savings, such as a 401(k)

Unfortunately, the retirement landscape has changed. Due diligence is placed on employees to invest and save for retirement versus the golden years where relying on a pension was the norm. And with constant threats of Social Security going away or benefits being reduced, one cannot rely solely on social programs, such as Social Security, to retire comfortably. In the next few sections, I will detail the top reasons why a 401(k) is vital for a financially secure retirement.

Reason 1: Fewer Companies Are Offering Pensions

In today's economic climate, fewer companies are offering pensions. Unlike a 401(k), where the employee must make monthly financial contributions, a pension is entirely funded by the employer. A pension offers guaranteed automatic payouts in retirement based on a formula that considers your compensation and years of service at a company. The longer your tenure and the more you make, the higher your automatic payouts. Pensions come with security and peace of mind, as they are not subject to market fluctuations and turmoil like a 401(k) plan is.

Pensions place the burden of funding one's retirement on the employer. On the other hand, 401(k) plans put the financial funding of retirement on you, the employee. With 401(k) plans, not only is the financial burden placed on you, but the consequences of making bad investments or maybe even outliving the amount you've saved in your 401(k) are put on your plate as well. In recent years, the funding of one's retirement has moved from pension plans to 401(k) plans, with the primary reason being the expense employers are burdened with when offering pensions to their employees. But unfortunately, for 401(k) plans to be beneficial, one must make contributions. This is where problems begin to arise, as many are struggling with debt, can barely manage their day-to-day bills, and are simply too cash strapped to allocate money to their retirement plans.

Many have postponed contributing to their 401(k) and have instead focused on more immediate financial needs. Unfortunately, putting retirement on the back burner has serious consequences, such as delaying the age you're able to retire. Instead of retiring at sixty-two, you may have to work into your seventies and eighties because postponing 401(k) contributions means you miss out on one of the critical drivers of wealth: compound interest.

Reason 2: You Can't Rely on Social Security

To understand why you can't rely on Social Security during retirement, you first need to know why Social Security benefits were created. On August 14, 1935, President Franklin D. Roosevelt signed the Social Security Act, which launched the creation of Social Security benefits that were to serve as a federal safety net for the elderly, unemployed, and disadvantaged.[11]

The signing of this act was brought on by the widespread suffering and poverty caused by the Great Depression. The Great Depression and its economic toll brought hardship, homelessness, and hunger to millions of Americans. In cities across the country, shantytowns sprung up, soup kitchens offering free or low-cost food became common, the rate of suicide increased, and incidences of malnutrition and diet-related diseases, such as rickets, skyrocketed. In response to this calamity, President Roosevelt vowed to put a social insurance program in place to buffer the misery and distress experienced during the Great Depression.

In addition to serving as a federal safety net for the elderly, unemployed, and disadvantaged, a significant provision of the Social Security Act was creating a program to provide workers ages sixty-five and older with continuing income upon retiring. This program was to be financed by a payroll tax on employers and employees. This component of the Social Security Act is what we refer to today as Social Security retirement benefits. Since being signed into law in 1935, wide-sweeping changes have been made to the Social Security Act. When it comes to Social Security retirement benefits, specific changes have been made, such as benefit amounts being increased and the eligibility age being decreased from sixty-five to sixty-two.

Now that you know why Social Security benefits were brought about, you probably want to know how Social Security retirement benefits work. Remember, Social Security is designed to provide retirement support for American workers who pay into the system.[12] You pay Social Security taxes with every paycheck you earn. This tax money goes into a trust fund that pays benefits to:

- People who are currently retired
- People who become disabled
- Survivors of workers who have died
- Dependents of beneficiaries

If there is money left over after all of these categories of Social Security recipients have been paid, this unused portion is kept on reserve in the Social Security trust fund. Each year you work, you get credits to become eligible for benefits when it is your turn to retire. When you become eligible for benefits, you can collect benefits instead of paying for the benefits of others.

In recent years, there have been rumors of Social Security benefits going away. As a nation, we are having fewer children and are living longer. These two factors have worked in tandem to create a decline in the worker-to-beneficiary ratio. The balance has tipped to where fewer people are putting money into the Social Security system and more people are taking money out. As a result of this imbalance, the Social Security Administration forecasts the retirement program's costs will exceed the tax revenue it has coming in around 2021. At this point, Social Security will begin to dip into its trust fund reserves. This "dipping" is expected to continue until 2035, at which point it is forecasted that all money in the trust fund reserves will be exhausted.[13]

When this trust fund is depleted, Social Security retirement benefits will not "go away" or "go to zero," but rather, benefits will be reduced. After all, when you retire in your sixties, there will be people younger than you paying into the Social

Security system. Continuing taxes are expected to be enough to pay seventy-six percent of scheduled retirement benefits, which is the worst-case scenario. There is plenty of time for the government to step in and put initiatives in place to prevent this from happening, such as increasing taxes, decreasing benefits, or increasing the age at which people can start collecting Social Security retirement benefits.

But even if the government is able to step in and ensure you are paid your full Social Security retirement benefits, relying solely on these benefits would have one living slightly above the poverty line and struggling to pay for basic necessities, like health care and food. Social Security retirement benefits should be a resource to help one during retirement, not a resource that does all the heavy lifting. Social Security retirement benefits were only designed to replace forty percent of an average worker's salary. Most retirees who are currently receiving Social Security retirement benefits get around $1,500 a month, which is barely enough to make ends meet.

Retirees who have no 401(k) or pension and rely solely on Social Security during their retirement must live with roommates or in subsidized housing to lower their living costs, can barely afford groceries, and are constantly worrying about unplanned day-to-day expenses and medical bills popping up. If you want to live comfortably during retirement, you must begin contributing to a 401(k). It will provide you with the financial backing to confidently go into retirement while minimizing your dependence on social programs and will ensure you don't have to worry about whether Social Security retirement benefits will be around when you retire. Money from the government will be the icing on the cake rather than the entire cake itself.

How Does a 401(k) Build Wealth?

The sooner you start saving for retirement, the longer your money can sit and grow. For illustrative purposes, let's say you are twenty-five years old, making $45,000 annually, and you decide to contribute six percent of your pre-tax earnings to your 401(k). Assuming an annual return rate of 7%, when you retire at the age of sixty-five, you could have amassed $559,241 in retirement savings after forty years.

CONTRIBUTING TO 401(K) AT 25

Percent to Contribute	6%
Annual Salary	$45,000
Current Age	25
Age of Retirement	65
Current 401(k) Balance	$0
Annual Rate of Return	7%
Total Employee Contribution	$108,000
Total at Retirement	$559,241

Now, let's look at what happens when you delay contributing to your retirement. Let's say you put off contributing to your 401(k) until you are thirty-five with a more stable, higher-paying job. With an estimated annual return rate of 7%, contributing six percent of a higher salary of $65,000 could potentially leave you with only $382,221 in your retirement account at the age of sixty-five.

CONTRIBUTING TO 401(K) AT 35

Percent to Contribute	6%
Annual Salary	$65,000
Current Age	35
Age of Retirement	65
Current 401(k) Balance	$0
Annual Rate of Return	7%
Total Employee Contribution	$117,000
Total at Retirement	$382,221

When you delay contributions to your 401(k), you miss out on compound interest. Compound interest is one of the fundamentals of wealth, as it allows your money to snowball due to the interest it accrues.

What Is Compound Interest?

Compound interest, also known as "interest on interest," is a financial concept that can make or cost you money depending on whether you're the one doing the earning or paying. The concept behind compound interest is that interest you earn is added back to the principal sum of the loan or deposit. Because the interest you earn is added back to the principal, the balance doesn't just simply grow but, instead, multiplies at an increasing rate. This definition is probably really confusing, so let's illustrate it.

Let's say you make a deposit of $1,000 into an account with a 5% interest rate that is compounded annually. This $1,000 deposit would lead to you gaining fifty dollars in interest after the first year, bringing your balance to $1,050. The following year is when the magic of compound interest would kick in. Instead of accruing interest on the initial $1,000 deposit, you would instead gain interest on the $1,050 balance. The year after that, instead of earning interest on $1,050, you would gain interest on the $1,102.50 balance.

YEARS	FUTURE VALUE	TOTAL CONTRIBUTIONS
Year 0	$1,000	$1,000
Year 1	$1,050	$1,000
Year 2	$1,102.50	$1,000
Year 3	$1,157.63	$1,000
Year 4	$1,215.51	$1,000
Year 5	$1,276.28	$1,000
Year 6	$1,340.10	$1,000
Year 7	$1,407.10	$1,000
Year 8	$1,477.46	$1,000
Year 9	$1,551.33	$1,000
Year 10	$1,628.89	$1,000

This is where wealth creation begins. With compound interest, you earn interest on your initial deposit, and you also earn interest on the interest you just received. So even if you don't make any additional deposits, your earnings dramatically accelerate.

Here's an idea of how compound interest could grow your savings. A deposit of $1,000 at a 5% interest rate compounded annually for forty years with no additional deposits could increase to $7,039.99. Imagine that! A $1,000 deposit turning into $7,039.99 with no extra work on your end. Now, for some, $7,000 is a trivial amount of money. So let's play around with some more significant numbers. Imagine what your account would look like if you increased the initial deposit amount from $1,000 to $5,000. This increase of a few thousand dollars would potentially leave you with $35,199.94 after forty years.

What Are the Benefits of Contributing to a 401(k)?

In addition to leaving you with a cushy nest egg when it's time to retire, there are quite a few benefits associated with contributing to your 401(k). First and foremost, going with a traditional 401(k), where contributions are made with your pre-tax dollars, lowers your taxable income. Decreasing your taxable income means you pay less taxes. As if this isn't incentive enough, in many cases there are additional perks that may be offered by your employer to further entice you to contribute towards your 401(k). In the next few sections, we'll explore these benefits in greater detail.

Benefit #1: Employer Contribution Matching

When an employer matches your 401(k), they contribute to your retirement savings plan based on the amount of your contribution. There are several ways your contributions can be matched. The most common way is for employers to match a percentage of employee contributions, up to a certain amount.

Take the case of an employee whose annual gross pay is $65,000 and whose employer matches up to six percent of their 401(k) contributions. Let's say this employee decides to contribute six percent of their income to their 401(k). The employee's contribution would come out to $3,900 (six percent of their gross pay), and since their employer matches up to six percent of its employees' contributions, they would get $3,900 from their employer toward their 401(k). If the employee decides to contribute more than $3,900, they won't receive any additional funds from their employer since their employer only matches up to six percent of the employee's contribution. By comparison, if this employee only contributes four percent of their gross pay ($2,600), they would only receive $2,600 in employer contributions, leaving $1,300 on the table.

An employee contribution match is basically free money. To maximize its benefit and leave no money on the table, you should, at a minimum, contribute what your employer matches if this benefit is extended to you. That extra thousand or so from your employer may seem trivial, but combined with compound interest, your payoff will be monumental when it comes time to retire.

If you are twenty-five years old, getting paid $45,000 annually, and making contributions of six percent with an employer who matches contributions of up to six percent, you're potentially looking at $1,118,482 when you retire at sixty-five, assuming a 7% annual rate of return. Without employer contributions, you'd only earn $559,241.

Benefit #2: Decreases Taxable Income

Another critical advantage of contributing to a 401(k) is that it decreases your taxable income. With a traditional 401(k), your contributions are made pre-tax, so these amounts are not included in your taxable income for the year. Let's say your salary is $70,000, and you contribute six percent of it to a traditional tax-deferred 401(k). Thanks to these contributions, your taxable income becomes $65,800. Sheltering your taxable income from taxation allows you to lower your tax bill.

Barriers Most Face When It Comes to Saving for Retirement

You'd think with all the benefits associated with 401(k) plans, everyone would be contributing toward them, but this isn't the case. The reality is not all people have access to 401(k) retirement savings plans, and those with access don't understand how 401(k) plans work, don't have the funds to begin contributing, or have other things going on, such as excessive optimism or cynicism, that prevent them from utilizing this resource. In the next few sections, we'll explore some of the most common barriers faced when it comes to saving for retirement.

Barrier #1: No Access to a 401(k)

Not everyone has access to a 401(k). Don't despair if you fall into this category. You still have several options for funding your retirement, such as:

- **Roth IRA (Individual Retirement Account):** A Roth IRA is a retirement account that allows you to contribute your already-taxed dollars. With this retirement plan, your money grows tax free, and your withdrawals during retirement are tax free as well. As of 2021, the Roth IRA annual contribution limit is $6,000. If you are fifty or older, you can contribute $7,000.
- **Traditional IRA:** A traditional IRA is a retirement savings plan that allows you to contribute your pre-tax dollars to a retirement account, where it grows tax deferred until you begin making withdrawals during retirement. As of 2021, the traditional IRA contribution limit is $6,000. Those fifty or older can contribute $7,000.
- **SEP IRA:** A Simplified Employee Pension (SEP) IRA is a type of traditional IRA retirement account that gives tax breaks to business owners and self-employed individuals who want to put money away for the future. As of 2021, SEP IRA annual contribution limits cannot exceed the lesser of twenty-five percent of compensation or $58,000.
- **Investment Account:** Stop thinking you're limited to saving for your retirement in a retirement account. If your job doesn't give you access to a 401(k), you've maxed out your traditional or Roth IRA, or you don't meet the eligibility requirements for a SEP IRA, consider putting money away

in a regular investment account. Sure, you miss out on the employer contribution matching benefits associated with 401(k) plans and the tax benefits that come with IRAs, but a standard investment account has a lot of flexibility, no age restrictions for taking money out, and no contribution limits associated with them.

Barrier #2: Can Barely Afford Everyday Expenses

Many can't contribute to retirement because they can barely afford to pay their everyday bills. If you're in this boat, maxing out retirement contributions isn't going to be feasible; in fact, until you increase your income, it's going to be impossible, but that doesn't mean you can't save something for the future.

Let's say you are twenty-five years old, making $45,000 annually, and decide to set aside a mere one percent of your salary toward your 401(k). Assuming a 7% annual rate of return, you could be sitting on $93,207 after four decades. If you have an employer that matches your contributions, you're potentially looking at $186,414 when it comes time to retire.

Many people are discouraged from saving for retirement because they feel their small contributions don't make a difference, but even if you steadily save a small amount, over time, it will go a long way.

Barrier #3: Excessive Optimism

Some people don't invest in their future due to emotionally founded reasons, such as excessive optimism. Believe it or not, many people expect something great to happen in their lives that will eliminate the need to save for retirement. Some believe they are going to marry rich, inherit money, or start an incredibly successful business that will make up for their lack of retirement readiness. It's good to be optimistic; however, these events rely on hope, promise, and future events—none of which are guaranteed.

Barrier #4: Cynicism

The opposite of optimism is cynicism, which can derail one's retirement readiness as well. Some have such a negative outlook on life that they don't feel the need to save for retirement. They think the world will end or they will be dead and not around to reap the benefits of saving for retirement in forty to fifty years. With such negative views, it's easy to adopt a "What's the point?" attitude toward retirement.

What's worse are those who succumb to the "You Only Live Once" (YOLO) mantra. These people live in the moment and want to enjoy life now because, deep down, they have negative views on what the future may hold. Instead of putting money away for retirement, which is so many years away, they focus on the "now" and funnel their money toward vacations, fine dining, and luxury goods. It's not wrong to invest in these things, but if you treat yourself to these finer luxuries and have no money stashed away for retirement, there's a problem.

Barrier #5: Lack of Education

The reality is most people are not educated on what a 401(k) is and how it fits into their retirement plan. What's worse, employers who offer 401(k) plans to their employees have done a terrible job of educating them on the actual benefits.

At a glance, it's difficult to understand the benefits of contributing to a 401(k). Without proper education, saving for retirement becomes a burden rather than a wealth-building opportunity. This lack of education and understanding causes many to forgo the use of their employer-sponsored 401(k).

An Additional Note on 401(k) Plans

Be Wary of Making Early Withdrawals from Your 401(k)

Once you start contributing to your 401(k) and it begins growing in value, it can be tempting to get your hands on this money, especially when immediate financial needs arise. Whether it be a down payment for a house, college tuition, or even an unexpected financial emergency, it's important to proceed very carefully when considering a 401(k) withdrawal. There are steep consequences associated with withdrawing funds from 401(k) plans before the age of fifty-nine-and-a-half. The government considers a 401(k) as a tool strictly for retirement funding, not a savings account or emergency savings fund you can use to get through hard times. If you withdraw funds before you reach the age of fifty-nine-and-a-half, you'll owe both income taxes on the amount you withdraw, as well as an additional ten percent early distribution penalty tax.

After paying taxes and penalties, the amount you withdraw is cut almost in half.

Early withdrawals also mean you're missing out on compound interest. Let's say you make a withdrawal of $20,000 from your 401(k) that has an average return of 7% per year. If you withdraw $20,000 at the age of thirty-five with plans to retire at sixty-two, you won't have $20,000 less when you retire; the potential future value of your $20,000 today could be $124,277 by the time you reach retirement age in twenty-seven years. Let me break it down for you: That $20,000 early withdrawal would cause you to miss out on $124,277 when it comes time to retire.

Withdrawing from your 401(k) when you are cash-strapped seems like a great idea. Unlike relying on credit cards, there is no interest involved, nor is there the embarrassment of turning to family or friends. However, be sure to exhaust all options before withdrawing from your 401(k), as based on the calculations we've run, it simply isn't worth it, and the consequences are tremendous.

Conclusion

Retirement savings is a delicate topic for many. Most of us have negative feelings associated with the financial aspects of retirement. Many of us have watched our parents and grandparents struggle with not having enough money saved for retirement to sustain their livelihood. Others have watched their parents lose their savings and investments during The Great Recession. This has led to many developing an independent attitude toward their finances, preferring self-created savings versus "risky" options like a 401(k) to facilitate retirement readiness.

Unlike traditional savings accounts, 401(k) plans harness

compound interest, which allows those who utilize them to exponentially stretch their dollars. A 401(k) combined with other wealth-building strategies outlined in this book will ensure you have more than enough to financially sustain yourself during retirement and, in some cases, enough left over for the generations that come after you.

Activity

Many people delay planning for retirement because they think of it as a period where they'll sit around the house idly twiddling their thumbs, when, in fact, retirement should be thought of as a second act, where you have complete control over how you spend your time. If planned correctly, retirement can be a period of your life where you travel all the time, volunteer, become a key figure in your community, spend time with family and friends, and live life fully to your heart's content, with no financial stress holding you back. After all, you've had your whole life to plan, save, and prep for this moment.

As explained in this chapter, many put retirement planning on the back burner, which is why, for this chapter's activity, we're going to get a head start on retirement planning by making a retirement vision board. During this activity, you want to think big!

Materials Needed

- Any kind of board (a pinboard, corkboard, or simple poster board)
- Magazines to cut images and quotes from that align with your retirement goals

- Images and text from artwork, old books, computer printouts, etc.
- Scissors
- Glue sticks or double-sided tape
- Paper and pen
- Markers
- Mementos and/or photos of things that inspire you
- Any type of art supplies that bring you joy, such as watercolors, stickers, or crayons

Include pictures on your board that illustrate how you want to feel during retirement. Include images of what you want to do or items you wish to have. If your dream is to backpack through Europe, include pictures of the most beautiful cities and tourist spots in Europe. If you want to spend your retirement taking month-long road trips throughout the United States, include images of an RV, campsites, and destinations you'd like to explore.

Use scissors to cut out pictures from magazines, or you can even print images from your computer and glue them on your board. Add in some favorite quotes or words to make a board that reflects your values. When you've completed your retirement vision board, don't just stash it away in your closet or garage; it is imperative you keep this board someplace where you'll see it daily and be inspired.

Now that you've made your retirement vision board, it's time to start working to make these dreams a reality. You've got all these big plans for an event happening ten, twenty, or even thirty years from now, but what will you do in the present moment to make your retirement vision board your reality?

I'll give you a clue: Start contributing to that 401(k).

RULE # 7

Diversify Your Streams of Income

When starting out on your wealth journey, you will more than likely be in a financial situation where your household income comes from your nine-to-five. In this scenario, you trade your time and efforts for money, and the amount of money you earn is dependent on the skill sets you possess. This setup is satisfactory for most, but it shouldn't be for you.

For ages, we have depended on our day jobs as the primary mechanism for building wealth and the principal source of our household income; however, relying so heavily on your day job is dangerous. After all, job security is an illusion. When you rely solely on your day job for income, you are just a phone call or pink slip away from falling on hard times. Diversifying your income streams mitigates this risk.

In addition to mitigating the risks associated with job insecurity, diversifying your streams of income is also a way to aggressively tackle your financial goals. The additional money coming from your newfound streams of income can be applied to different financial goals to allow you to reach wealth faster. Whether you are trying to get out of debt, save for retirement, buy a house, or build an emergency savings fund, diversifying your income streams will turn these goals into a not-so-distant reality.

What Does It Mean to Diversify Your Income?

The majority of people don't have diversified income streams and are over-reliant on one source of income, which, when you boil it down, means their income allocation is riddled with uncertainty and risk. The good news? This over-reliance on one source of income is a common situation that can easily be remedied with income diversification. To diversify your income, you simply need to engage in different activities, each generating a separate stream of income.

The goal is to get to a place where you have income from your day job, a side hustle, and various sources of passive income streams, such as dividend and interest income. The logic is that your day job's income will not be affected by what is happening with your side hustle, which should not be affected by your dividend or interest income, as each stream of income is independent.

What Streams of Income Exist?

In the following section, we will detail the seven different types of income streams almost all millionaires have that you should strive to have to build wealth.

Income Stream #1: Earned Income

Earned income is money you earn in exchange for your time, efforts, and skill set. A dental hygienist who is paid hourly or an account manager who is on a salary both receive earned income. You don't have to invest your personal capital to receive earned income, and your earnings are predictable. With earned income, you know you will get paid a set amount every few weeks.

Most people stick to this income stream, as it is a comfortable place to be mentally and carries little risk. But unfortunately, this comfort leads to complacency that prevents one from discovering new opportunities. For instance, you may have a kick-ass lawyer who earns a lucrative salary that allows him to live a comfortable lifestyle. Since they've been a lawyer for years, they have probably gotten really good at being a lawyer, so this job might bring them little stress on a day-to-day basis. That comfort might deter this kick-ass lawyer from opening their own private law firm.

Additionally, earned income has limited potential. There are only so many hours in the day an employee can work, and there are only so many rungs you can climb up a corporate ladder. This severely limits the amount of money you're able to make with earned income. Detaching yourself from this income stream is difficult, if not impossible; however, this detachment or shift from relying solely on earned income is necessary. Earned income requires a ton of time while providing unsubstantial and limited payout.

Income Stream #2: Profit Income

Profit income is money you earn by selling services or goods at a higher price than it costs you to deliver. This income stream requires entrepreneurship and business management skills to be successful. It also requires substantial investments of time and money but typically only in the initial stages. Many working a nine-to-five job would love to incorporate this income stream into their portfolio but become apprehensive due to the risk.

Income Stream #3: Interest Income

Interest income is money earned in the form of interest that has accumulated on investments. Examples of interest income include money earned from a certificate of deposit or money earned from lending money to the government in the form of Treasury Bills. Savings accounts and dividends also generate interest income.

Many doubt the effectiveness of interest income due to the low rates of return associated with it, but when you factor in the power of compound interest and the minimal risk involved, it pays to dabble in this form of income.

Income Stream #4: Dividend Income

Dividend income is money you get as a return on company shares you own. When you purchase stocks from a company, you "own" a piece of the company and become one of its shareholders. When companies have earnings, they can do a few things, such as use the earnings to expand operations, pay debt, or stockpile cash. They can also choose to distribute this profit to shareholders, whether it be in the form of cash or stock. This distribution of profit to shareholders is called a dividend. Dividends can be paid out monthly, quarterly, or annually, although annually is most common.

Income Stream #5: Rental Income

Rental income is money you receive for letting someone use or occupy your property. With rental income, revenue is generated from the difference in what you invested in the property versus what you are renting it out for. This is a very lucrative source of income, but it requires a significant amount of money up front, which is a barrier to entry for many.

Income Stream #6: Capital Gains

Capital gains are earned as a result of selling a capital asset, such as stocks, bonds, or real estate, for more than what you purchased it for. An example of a capital gain would be buying a house for $250,000 and selling it for $350,000.

Income Stream #7: Royalty Income

Royalty income is earned from the use of your artistic works, literary works, or patents. With royalty income, someone else makes a profit off the use of your product. They make the revenue and pay you a small percentage of what they earn. In music, royalties are paid to copyrighted music owners for its use, while in art, royalties may be paid for the use of images.

Royalties can be negotiated in a variety of ways. You can sell your work to an investor for the promise of a constant percentage of royalties on the revenue the investor makes, or you can receive royalties any time someone uses your work. The latter example is called licensing.

Passive vs. Active Income

These income streams, whether it be earned, profit, interest, dividend, rental, capital gains, or royalty, lie on a spectrum, with active and passive income being on opposite ends. Passive income comes from regularly received cash flow that requires minimal to no effort or oversight to maintain. Passive income is achieved when you put your money to work for you.

With passive income, you may have to put significant time and effort into getting started, but after a while, the money flows with little effort. Simply put, passive income allows you to continue getting paid after the work is done. Dividend income is an excellent example of passive income. After the initial purchase of dividend-paying stocks, there isn't much you have to do beyond checking how your investments are performing. Additional forms of passive income include selling e-books or investing in rental and Airbnb properties. Flipping the balance of the scale to where passive income provides more of your earnings should be one of your financial goals. I'll even go as far as saying you haven't reached financial independence until all your living expenses can be paid for by your passive income.

On the other hand, active income is defined as income that comes from active efforts to earn money. A traditional nine-to-five is a source of active income. Active income can also come from a side hustle, such as braiding hair or driving with Uber. With active income, you must do something to earn money, and it requires either a significant amount of time or effort. Jobs associated with active income can be either physically or mentally challenging—sometimes both! With passive income, you earn money without having to continuously work for it. Money flows to you, whether you are sleeping, on vacation, or sick. With active income, you consistently work for your money. If you do not work, you do not get paid.

Many people do just fine relying solely on active income; however, if you are looking to transition from doing "just fine" to thriving, you need to incorporate passive streams of income into your income diversification strategy. If done right and planned accordingly, you can gradually replace your active income with passive income. When these efforts are made consistently and strategically, you'll get to the point where you can work fewer hours or stop working your nine-to-five altogether.

But here's the thing: This is not a journey for the impatient. With active income, you go to work, and two weeks later, your check is guaranteed. With passive income, it can take a while before you are consistently earning income, and it can take years before your passive income earnings can replace the income from your nine-to-five.

How to Get Started with Income Diversification

Many are under the impression that when it comes to diversifying their income streams, they're going to get a rental property, start drop-shipping, or even start investing, and two weeks later, they're going to be making an additional $30,000 a month in passive income. I'm sorry to break it to you, but it doesn't work that way. The shift to having diversified sources of income requires long-term vision. To be successful, you should seek small amounts of income from different sources, whether it be earned, profit, interest, dividend, rental, capital gains, or royalty income, with a long-term goal of having more passive income coming in than active.

Let's start off by looking at the most common source of income, your nine-to-five job, and ensuring you have maximized your income in this category.

Is Your Income Optimized?

I would first start off by examining whether you are making the maximum amount of money you can make with your skill sets at your current employer. If you are giving one hundred percent and, after doing research, find you are being underpaid, it's time to ask for a raise. If your employer cannot meet your request for a raise, it's time to update your LinkedIn profile and look for another job. There is no point in staying at a job where you are not valued.

Is Your Behavior Optimized? What about Your Performance?

If your work ethic is lacking and you're performing sub-optimally, say at seventy-five percent, it's time to assess the areas you can improve on. This might mean improving your relationship with your boss or coworkers or reassessing your attitude, work ethic, production levels, etc.

Now, you're probably wondering why I am advising you to dedicate time and energy to your nine-to-five when it's a stream of active income I told you to gradually disassociate yourself from just a few pages ago. I've noticed throughout the years that some mistakenly assume when they're not performing at their nine-to-five, the solution is to become their own boss by starting a business. This thought process has led to a lot of failed entrepreneurs. Consider your nine-to-five as a boot camp on someone else's dime for you to hone in on your customer service, communication, expectation setting, and service delivery skills. Until you have mastered these skills, you should hold off on investing your time and money in your own business.

Let's say you have a tardiness problem. If you're guaranteed a paycheck every two weeks but still can't motivate yourself to get to work on time, I doubt you will be able to change this behavior when you launch a business venture where the first few years you're barely breaking even and are bleeding money. You will be that annoying business owner who is always opening their shop late or failing to meet agreed-upon deadlines.

If you've been given feedback time and time again that you come across as standoffish or even combative, it wouldn't be wise to quit and start your own company dealing face-to-face with potential customers and business partners all day. Your attitude would turn them off. Instead, take some time to work on your demeanor and delivery while working at your nine-to-five job, then launch your own company.

Are You Taking Advantage of All Perks and Benefits Offered by Your Employer?

Make use of all the benefits offered by your employer. If your employer offers a 401(k) match, make sure you contribute, at minimum, what they match. If your employer offers tuition reimbursement, as long as it aligns with your long-term goals, consider taking advantage of this, whether you obtain a bachelor's degree, master's degree, or PhD. Some employers even go the extra mile in supporting their employees if they decide to pursue career-advancing certifications, such as the Project Management Professional (PMP) certification or Six Sigma Green Belt (SSGB). These certifications can add $10,000 to $12,000 to one's salary, with costs ranging from $2,000 to $4,000. A lot of employers completely cover the costs associated with these career-advancing certifications.

There's a reason your employer is willing to invest in continuing education for its employees; it advances the workforce and sharpens its employees. Take part in these continuing education perks. Utilize them to advance your career, but don't forget to apply them to your side hustles and entrepreneurship ventures.

Get a Side Hustle

A side hustle is a great way to earn income outside of your day job. A side hustle can be a second job and, in some cases, a temporary or contract job, such as delivering for Postmates or driving for Uber. Some even use side hustles to scratch their entrepreneurial itch by starting a small business. Starting a business as a side hustle while having a full-time job can be a great way to mitigate the risks associated with entrepreneurship while allowing you to take baby steps toward becoming an entrepreneur. You can start any kind of business as a side hustle, from baking gluten-free dog treats to designing custom websites to starting a catering company.

Side hustles are a great way to improve your finances with the extra money they bring in. The money coming from your side hustle shouldn't go toward your discretionary income or "spending money." Instead, these earnings should go toward your sinking funds, retirement accounts, investments, or debt payments. The next few sections will serve as a basic framework for starting a side hustle for those looking to scratch their entrepreneurial itch.

Step 1: Brainstorm ideas.

Get your creative juices flowing by brainstorming ideas for your side hustle.

- **What are you good at?** If you're good at math and love kids, you could tutor a few kids in the evenings and on the weekends as a math tutor. If you're an excellent cook, you can start meal prepping for those who are too busy to cook for themselves.
- **What are you passionate about?** What hobbies do you devote yourself to in your spare time? If you are passionate about working out, you could start personal training or teach fitness classes at your local gym in your spare time. If you love social media and have a ton of likes and followers, you can provide consulting services to people and brands looking to increase their social media reach and engagement.
- **What processes frustrate you?** What issues do you face in your everyday life you feel could be improved with a business idea? For example, if you're frustrated by the lack of dog groomers in your neighborhood, others might be disappointed as well. If there's enough demand, you could start your own dog grooming business to fill the void.

The possibilities are truly endless when it comes to these types of ventures. Specific examples of side hustles you can undertake as an entrepreneur include:

- Virtual Assistant
- Home Inspector
- Personal Chef
- Housekeeper
- Dog Walker
- Lawn Care
- Baby-Sitting
- Interior Design
- Auto Repair
- Home Daycare
- Meal Planning
- E-Commerce Store
- Video Production
- Travel Planning
- Event Planning
- Personal Trainer
- Graphic Designer
- Tour Guide
- Laundry Service

Step 2: Narrow it down.

Narrow your list down to three ideas and conduct further research on them, keeping the following points in mind:

- How are others making money doing this?

- What are the barriers to entry?
- What work would be required from you?
- What time commitment would be needed from you?
- What are the initial startup costs?
- How much money do you project to make realistically in three months? Six months? One year? Three years?

Step 3: Decide on the idea you're going to pursue.

After you've narrowed your list down to three side hustles you'd be interested in pursuing, it's time to narrow it down to just one.

Step 4: Don't jump in just yet!

You've narrowed it down to one idea, but it's still too soon to jump in. It's time to do some additional research. Thanks to social media and the worldwide web, it's now super easy to get a glimpse of your soon-to-be competitors' business strategies, audience, and business models.

Let's say you decide to offer bicycle repair services as your side hustle. A search of "bicycle repair" in your web browser will quickly populate bicycle repair companies in your area. From there, you can browse through each company's website and explore sections, such as "What We Do," "Services Offered," or "Our Guarantee," to get an idea of how they stand out in the marketplace. They may even have a "Pricing" section on their website, which will gauge how much you can charge without coming across as too cheap or too expensive.

Most of the time, they'll have their social media pages linked on their website. You can browse through their followers to get an idea of the demographic of clientele attracted to their brand, which will give you a head start when it comes to your own branding and marketing.

Step 5: Create a business plan.

A business plan serves as a guide that helps get you through each stage of starting and managing your side hustle. Your business plan will serve as a roadmap for structuring, running, and growing your side hustle. There is no right or wrong way to write your business plan, so long as the plan you create meets your needs. Questions to get your creative juices flowing when writing your business plan include:

- What are some common problems people in need of your product or service face on a day-to-day basis?
- Without your product or service, how are these problems being solved?
- How will your product or service solve these problems?
- How is your product or service superior to the solutions your potential customers currently have in place?
- What is your value proposition?
- How are you different from others who offer a similar product or service?
- What advantage do you have when it comes to your product or service that your competitors cannot easily replicate?
- How will you get the word out about your business?
- How will you conduct customer outreach?

- What are some characteristics of your ideal customer?
- What metrics will you utilize to gauge your side hustle's performance?
- How much will you charge for your product or service?
- Based on the price you've set for your product or service, how many customers do you need to work with to make a profit on a daily, weekly, and monthly basis?
- What costs will you incur starting this venture?

Getting Started with Passive Income

You've optimized the income from your nine-to-five, and you've started a side hustle to bring in some extra cash. It's now time to focus on passive income. As stated earlier, there are various forms of passive income. A detailed strategy for tackling this income stream would take an entire book, so we're going to narrow it down to the easiest passive income stream with the lowest barrier to entry: investing in dividend stocks.

What Are Dividend Stocks?

Dividend stocks are companies that pay shareholders a portion of earnings, also known as dividends, on a regular basis. These dividends are paid in cash and are paid either on a monthly, quarterly, or annual basis. These payments are funded by profits a company generates but doesn't need to retain to reinvest in the business. Not all companies are able to offer dividend stocks. For a company to even be able to offer dividend stocks, it must have a robust business model that consistently generates more profit than it needs to run. It also needs to not have a better use of those profits, such as reinvestment in the business, than returning them to shareholders.

Dividend stocks put money directly into the hands of shareholders. When you are paid a dividend, you have control over what you do with it. You can use the dividend to cover your living expenses, reinvest in more shares of the same stock, or invest in different stocks. For educational purposes, let's look at a few real-world examples of dividend-paying stocks. The first example is Realty Income Corporation (NYSE: O), whose stock is trading for approximately $51.65 per share at the time of this writing. The company pays dividends monthly. If you own Realty Income Corporation stock, you can expect to receive a cash payment of $0.233 every month for each share you own. Another example of a dividend-paying stock is Walmart (NYSE: WMT), whose stock is trading for approximately $124.65 per share at the time of this writing. Walmart pays dividends every quarter. If you own Walmart stock, you can expect to receive a cash payment of $0.54 each quarter for each share you own.

At a glance, getting paid $0.233 monthly for Realty Income Corporation stock or $0.54 quarterly for Walmart stock is laughable, but if you are consistently buying dividend-paying stocks to the point where you have thousands of dollars invested into these dividend-paying corporations, these cents quickly add up.

Now, let's be realistic. Will you be making substantial amounts of money off dividend stocks right away? No. But will you eventually get to a point where you are bringing in a few thousand or so in dividend income each month? Yes, so long as you remember that dividend investing is a marathon, not a sprint. In the next few sections, we'll review in detail how to get started with investing in dividend stocks.

Step 1: Choose your investing platform.

There was once a time when you had to pick up the phone, ask a broker to trade for you, and pay a hefty commission fee to buy stocks. We're now living in an age where you can buy and sell shares, bonds, funds, and investment trusts with just a few clicks of a mouse or taps on a screen, whether through a website or via an app. We are now in an era where you can engage in "do it yourself" investing.

To get started investing in dividend stocks, you simply need to begin purchasing dividend stocks. You have two options for buying dividend stocks: 1) purchase directly through the company or 2) purchase through a brokerage app. Technically speaking, the purchase of stocks directly from a company is not going to be one hundred percent direct. You will have to go through a transfer agent, such as Computershare, to purchase the stock. Buying the stock "directly" via a transfer agent means you won't have to open a brokerage account and no commissions are paid, so you get to keep more of your hard-earned money.

When purchasing stocks directly from a company, there may be a minimum investment amount ranging anywhere between twenty-five dollars to $500. The minimum investment amount is dependent on the corporation's policies and the price of each individual share. Not all companies allow the practice of "direct" stock purchases, but the few companies that do are:

- The Coca-Cola Company
- ExxonMobil
- Johnson & Johnson
- Walmart

- Altria Group

In addition to purchasing stocks directly, you can also use a brokerage app, such as:

- Robinhood
- Acorns
- Stash
- M1 Finance
- Stockpile
- TD Ameritrade Mobile

Online investing platforms are not free, and there is a variety of pricing structures used in this burgeoning industry. Some platforms charge an ongoing administrative fee, which is a percentage of your account balances, while others charge a flat fee either on a monthly or annual basis. There are a few that forgo administrative, monthly, or annual fees and instead charge fees every time you buy or sell stocks. When choosing a platform, you should research its pricing structure to ensure it will work with the type of investing you have in mind.

Step 2: Check out a pre-screened list.

In theory, dividend investing should be pretty straightforward; after all, you're merely buying stocks from companies that pay dividends. Unfortunately, there are a multitude of companies that pay dividends and many variables to consider when selecting stocks to buy.

To get started with buying dividend stocks, I would check out a pre-screened list, such as the S&P 500 Dividend Aristocrats list. This list is an excellent tool for filtering companies and narrowing your list down to the best dividend stocks you should purchase based on your investing goals. The following are the criteria and requirements a company must meet to be featured on this list:

- Must be a member of the S&P 500
- Must have increased dividends for twenty-five consecutive years
- Must have at least $3 billion in market capitalization
- Must have an average daily trading volume of at least $5 million

The S&P 500 Dividend Aristocrats list is reviewed annually, there are at least forty companies on the list, and the list is equally split between various industries and sectors. Another pre-screened list for dividend stocks worthy of mentioning is the Dividend Achievers list.

STEP 3: CONDUCT RESEARCH.

Check out all of the pre-screened lists I've recommended. Do research on the featured companies that stand out to you in regards to the frequency of their dividend payments and the amount, but don't stop your research at the payment amounts and frequency. You want to build your portfolio with stocks that are not too volatile or unpredictable when you're first getting started with dividend investing. The volatility of a stock is the fluctuation of price in any given time frame. When it comes to unpredictability, the stock market as a whole is unpredictable, but an unpredictable stock is riddled with unknowns. In addition to predictability and volatility, you should also consider the following:

- **Consistency:** If a company's profits are falling, they might resort to slashing or even eliminating dividend payments. Check to see if the company has a long history of paying dividends and whether there have been missed payments or decreased payout amounts in the past to gauge how consistent they have been.
- **Sustainability:** This one is going to take some digging. Still, you want to do research on the amount of debt the company carries, its share of the marketplace, and the advantages it holds over its competitors. Essentially, what makes this company stand apart that will allow it to continue making significant revenue for years to come?
- **Track record of growth:** You want to invest in dividend stocks that grow over time in terms of both share price and dividend.

All of the data you'll need to gather this information can be found via publicly reported quarterly earnings statements, annual reports, and a quick Google search. This isn't going to be a fun project, but it is necessary to ensure you purchase the best stocks for your investing goals.

Step 4: Make your decisions and purchase stock.

At this point, you've done research on different investing platforms and their pricing strategies. You have also done research on companies that pay dividends, including the frequency and amount. Now, it's time to set up an account with an investing platform, transfer money to it, and start buying dividend stocks. Remember, the dividends companies pay are only a few cents. To reach dividend payouts that are substantial enough to supplement your income, you need to consistently buy dividend stocks. I recommend carving out a few hundred dollars of your budget each month for this endeavor.

Conclusion

When it comes to diversifying one's income, the most significant barrier to entry is laziness. It doesn't take rocket science to see the benefits of having more than one source of income, but income diversification requires a certain level of dedication and discipline most don't inherently possess. It's easy to go to work for a set number of hours every day, be told exactly what is needed from you, know what specific dates you're going to get paid each month, and how much your paychecks will be.

Diversifying your income by incorporating a side hustle, starting a small business, or investing in stocks means temporarily adding uncertainty and risk to the mundane life you've grown accustomed to. You will eventually reap the fruits of your labor, but it will take time and require patience, which is where most fall off the wagon.

We are not accustomed to waiting. With a nine-to-five job, it takes a few weeks after getting hired to start receiving paychecks, whereas reaping the rewards of diversifying your income can take months to break even and years to start making a profit. It will take a lot of work, but it's a challenge you have to undertake. You can survive with one source of income, but you will not thrive.

To build wealth and reach the financial goals you've set for yourself, such as being debt-free, paying off all your student loans, or having a hefty savings account, you will need additional revenue streams outside of your day job.

Activity

In this chapter, we devoted quite a chunk of time to discussing dividend stocks. Investing in dividend stocks is a great way to bring in passive income. Buying them is easier than ever nowadays with the variety of trading and investment apps on the market.

For this chapter's activity, your job is to comb through the different investment platforms we've rounded up and educate yourself on their value proposition. This activity's objective is for you to become thoroughly educated on these apps, specifically the fees associated with using them, account requirements, such as minimum balances, promotions they may have going on, and the perks they offer to their users. Use the following chart to record your findings.

	VALUE PROPOSITION	FEES	PROMOTIONS	PERKS	ACCOUNT MINIMUM
Robinhood					
M1 Finance					
Acorns					
Stockpile					
TD Ameritrade Mobile					

RULE #8

Build Wealth with Equity Associated with Homeownership

After I graduated from college, I went through a phase where I would relocate to a different city on a whim. I moved from Atlanta to New York, New York to Miami, and when my wanderlust had finally dissipated, I made the trek from Miami back to Atlanta. I wasn't one hundred percent sure if my move to Atlanta was going to be a permanent one, so instead of renting an apartment and signing a lease, I decided to be a stereotypical millennial and move in with my parents, who lived a short forty-five minutes away from the city.

This setup was a godsend. It allowed me to pay down my debt and start saving, but I craved my independence. After getting my savings to an amount I was comfortable with, I decided to get an apartment. Unbeknownst to me, the Atlanta housing market had changed quite a bit since I'd moved away. For one, the rent was now outrageous. A one-bedroom apartment in the middle of the city was in the $1,300 to $1,600 price range compared to the $1,000 to $1,200 it had been years prior. I wasn't excited about the inflated rent, but I bit the bullet and was going to sign a lease until I met up with a close friend of mine for dinner one evening.

"Instead of renting an apartment, you should use some of your savings for a down payment and just buy a house," she suggested.

The idea of purchasing a home was so farfetched to me, yet the suggestion rolled so casually off her tongue. Instantly, my mind was flooded with a series of "I can't" thoughts. *I can't purchase a home; I'm single. I don't have enough money saved. There's no way I'd be able to afford a mortgage payment. I don't even know how to work a lawnmower.*

I explained my hesitation to my friend.

"You think you can't purchase a home because you aren't educated on purchasing a home," she told me.

She explained that she had a close friend who was a real estate agent and suggested I meet up with her to discuss homeownership, the buying process, and any misconceptions I had. A week later, I took her advice and met up with her friend for a coffee date. Two months later, I closed on my home.

You may be in the same mental space I was in a few years ago, where being a homeowner seems like a very distant reality. You may be mentally battling "I can't" thoughts that have prevented you from looking into homeownership. These thoughts may tempt you to skip this chapter, but I urge you to do otherwise. This chapter aims to educate you on how homeownership builds wealth so you can keep this top of mind as you set your long- and short-term wealth goals and go about making your day-to-day financial decisions.

How Does Homeownership Build Wealth?

Owning a home helps you build wealth—and most of the time, more efficiently and effectively than other methods. The recipe for building wealth through homeownership is as follows: Purchase a home in the right location, properly maintain it and build equity in the home. In fifteen to thirty years, sell the house at a higher price point than you paid for it or hold on to it and pass it, as well as its value, along to your children and grandchildren when you pass away.

Despite how clear this logic is, some people still question the validity of building wealth through homeownership, but the reality is if you don't buy a home, your only other option is to rent. Renting doesn't give you the opportunity to build equity. In a renting scenario, the only person who builds equity is the landlord, who funnels a portion of your rent payment toward paying the mortgage and keeps the rest as a profit. Still not convinced that homeownership builds wealth? In the following sections, we will explore the main concepts of building wealth through homeownership in greater detail.

Changes Financial Behaviors and Habits for the Better

One of the primary ways homeownership builds wealth is by changing your financial behaviors and habits for the better. To qualify for a home loan, you need to save for a down payment to cover a portion of the home's purchase price. Depending on the type of home loan you get, the down payment can vary from 3% to 20%.

A down payment comes from your personal savings and, in most cases, is paid in the form of cash, check, or electronic payment. The bigger your down payment, the less money you end up having to borrow. The remaining balance of the loan is paid off over time with regular installment payments, a.k.a your mortgage.

Let's say you've been diligently saving for a down payment for years and have managed to save $50,000. During the home-buying process, you find a beautiful, cozy cottage right outside the city limits for $250,000. As a result of saving $50,000, you'll only need to borrow $200,000, the latter of which you will be paying off with a thirty-year mortgage. So, how does this purchase build wealth? Well, first, saving $50,000 is not an insignificant feat. A goal of this magnitude takes years and requires significant dedication, resilience, and improvement of one's finances. This is where wealth creation begins. To reach this savings goal, you must change your financial behaviors for the better. You must diligently work to become more strategic with your day-to-day financial decisions and habits.

But it doesn't stop there. In addition to saving for a down payment, you will also need to get your credit score in tip-top shape. Your credit score dramatically influences your mortgage eligibility and the interest rate associated with your home loan; the higher your credit score, the lower your interest rate, and vice versa. As discussed earlier in this book, a credit score shows lenders your ability to repay debt, so for a purchase as big as a home, your poor credit might get you approved for a home loan but only at a high interest rate. Getting approved with a high interest rate costs you more in the long run and negates the wealth-building facets of homeownership. What's worse, a poor credit score might lead to you being denied for a home loan entirely. This will put you in a situation where you must continue renting instead of buying, which will also deny you access to the wealth-building benefits of homeownership.

Forced Savings

Another way homeownership builds wealth is by acting as a vehicle that causes forced savings. Forced savings is when an expense takes money out of your hands today and returns it to you years later in the form of an asset. Let's be honest: Diligently and regularly saving money is hard, especially in the consumer-centric world we live in. Ten percent of your monthly earnings is the recommended amount you should be saving, which most fail to do. Forced savings breaks this cycle.

When you purchase a home, you typically purchase it on a fifteen- or thirty-year term, with the term dictating the amount of time it will take you to fully pay off the loan. Let's say you purchase a home for $250,000 on a thirty-year term. After thirty years, the house is a $250,000 asset you own entirely. Consider this: If you had never purchased the home, would you have been able to save $250,000 during those thirty years? Probably not. $250,000 is a lot of money. The average person doesn't have the capacity or discipline to do this. On the other hand, a mortgage is an "expense" that is prioritized since the consequences of missing payments are dire.

You are "forced" to save every month if you want to keep a roof over your head. After thirty years of being "forced" to make these payments, you walk away with a $250,000 asset you own and can sell (possibly at a higher price than you paid for it).

Allows You to Build Equity

Home equity is the portion of your home you've paid off. It is the difference between what you owe on your mortgage and your home's worth. If your home is worth $210,000 and you owe $160,000 on your mortgage loan, you have $50,000 of equity.

Still confused as to how home equity works? Suppose you purchase a house for $210,000 and come up with a 10% down payment for your home's purchase price: $21,000. Your lender provides you with a mortgage loan of $189,000. If your home is appraised and found to be worth the $210,000 sales price, you now have $21,000 of equity, or $210,000 minus $189,000.

Jump ahead three years. You've been making your mortgage payments on time and now owe $180,000 on your mortgage. Maybe your home's value has jumped from $210,000 to $220,000 during this time. You now have $40,000 in equity, or $220,000 minus $180,000.

Two primary scenarios allow your home's equity to increase. In the first scenario, it increases as a result of you paying down the mortgage. In the second scenario, your home's equity increases as the value of your home jumps. Outside of these two equity-producing scenarios, you can proactively increase your home's equity by doing the following:

- **Increase your home's value by renovating and adding curb appeal.** Boost your home's worth by remodeling an outdated kitchen, adding a bathroom, or converting unused spaces, such as an attic, into a bedroom. Even small investments, such as investing in landscaping, switching to energy-efficient windows, or repainting the exterior of your home, can help as well.
- **Make more than the minimum monthly payments.** Paying more than the minimum monthly payment permits you to chip at the mortgage at a more aggressive rate.

An extra fifty dollars each month or even an additional payment each year that goes directly toward the principal balance goes a long way.
- **Follow the five-year rule.** You want to stay put in your home for a minimum of five years. No home is guaranteed to see its value jump, but generally, homeowners tend to get traction building equity around the five-year mark.

What Should and Shouldn't You Do with Equity?

This information is intriguing, but you're probably wondering how this relates to wealth. Equity is an essential financial tool and one of the most significant financial benefits of owning a home.

Let's say you are selling a home you have equity in. During the closing process, the purchaser will bring funds equal to your home's sale price. Those funds are used to pay off the following:

- The remaining balance of the mortgage
- Any home equity loans or home equity lines of credits (HELOCs) you may have
- Your closing costs, including agent commissions, taxes, etc.

If there's money left after those debts are paid in full, the remainder is paid out to you as a profit. The more equity you have in your home, the higher your profit.

You can even tap into home equity to eliminate your high-interest credit card debt or help cover your children's college tuition. How would you go about doing this? By borrowing money against the equity with a loan or line of credit. Whether you go the route of a loan or a line of credit, the house serves as collateral in both instances, which means it can be seized if you fail to make payments on the loan. Tapping into your home equity can be risky and detrimental if you go into it not fully understanding the repercussions. But while it's risky, there are some instances where a home equity loan or line of credit makes financial sense. Below are some dos and don'ts when it comes to home equity:

- **Do understand the risks involved.** A home equity line of credit decreases the amount of equity you have in your home. If you dip into your home's equity and the market value of your home drops, depending on how significant the drop, you can potentially lose all the equity you have in your home.
- **Do use home equity for home improvement projects that add value.** A home equity loan is most useful for home improvement projects that raise your home's resale value and entice prospective buyers.
- **Don't use home equity for non-essential expenses.** The small joys associated with purchases that are not only non-essential but also not strategic, such as designer clothing, the latest sports car, or temporary experiences like an extravagant family vacation, simply aren't worth it.
- **Don't dip into your home's equity if you plan on selling in the near future.** While you don't have to pay off your home equity loan or line of credit before you list your home for sale, you do need to have all debts related to your home paid by the time of closing.

- **Do use home equity to purchase other assets.** Home equity is an asset that should be used as a means to acquire other assets. For example, home equity can be used to purchase another property, so long as the property is income producing (turning the home into a bed-and-breakfast or renting the home out to long-term tenants).
- **Don't take out more than you need.** It's tempting to take out as much as you can when tapping into your home equity, but remember, your home is used as collateral. In a scenario where you take out too much or can't afford the repayments and default on the loan or line of credit, your home can be repossessed.

Buying vs. Renting

Yes, homeownership builds wealth, but there are some benefits to renting, the biggest being flexibility. The most common term for a lease or rental agreement is one year, and in some instances, you can get a lease for as short as six months. With renting, you can pack up and go as you please, but at the end of the day, flexibility is a non-financial benefit that, when stacked against the financial benefits of homeownership, really doesn't hold much weight. In the following sections, we will explore the reasons why homeownership is more advantageous than renting.

Renting Leads to No Changes in Financial Behavior

The barriers for renting an apartment are relatively low, which means there are little financial behaviors you'll need to change or financial dedication you'll need to adopt to rent. With renting, you miss out on the discipline and resilience you would garner by saving for a down payment. A month's rent and a security deposit are all one needs to rent an apartment. This runs from $2,000 to $2,500, depending on the city you live in. Coming up with $2,000 to $2,500 is trivial compared to the several thousand you would need to save for a down payment on a home.

Lower Net Worth

The net worth of homeowners significantly outpaces renters who, throughout their life, tend to accumulate little, if any, wealth. In fact, the only way a renter would be able to garner the same amount of wealth as a homeowner is if they were to invest an amount equal to a down payment in stocks, bonds, or assets and continue to add to this investment every month.

No Appreciation or Equity

Despite making monthly payments that might be equal to, or even more than, a mortgage payment, you miss out on appreciation and equity when you rent. The only person who reaps these financial gains in a renting scenario is the landlord you are renting from.

The property value of homes tend to appreciate, on average, 3% to 4% a year. Let's say you purchase a $250,000 home. At an appreciation rate of 4% a year, the home would be worth $260,000 after one year, a gain of $10,000. This appreciation occurs as you make payments each month toward your mortgage and gain equity in the home. The best part is the home is appreciating in value, not on the small initial down payment you made or monthly mortgage payments.

Rent Fluctuations

Anyone who has ever rented has experienced the dreaded rent increase that coincidentally occurs when it's time to renew your lease. In cities such as New York City, San Francisco, Oakland, and Boston, rent prices have increased at an unreasonable pace. This has made money tight for renters who are forced to spend more and more on housing. By purchasing a home at an affordable price point on a fixed-rate mortgage, your monthly payments are locked in at a cost that doesn't fluctuate.

You Throw Away Money

When you rent, it's basically wasted money. Now, some will say this statement is misleading; after all, when you rent, you pay money in exchange for a place to stay, so at the end of the day, the service requested has been granted. But if you look at the following chart, someone paying $1,500 for rent would have made $270,000 in rent payments after only fifteen years of renting with nothing to show for it.

HOW MUCH HAVE YOU THROWN AWAY ON RENT?

IF RENT IS	1 YEAR	5 YEARS	10 YEARS	15 YEARS
$1,500	$18,000	$90,000	$180,000	$270,000
$1,800	$21,600	$108,000	$216,000	$324,000
$2,000	$24,000	$120,000	$240,000	$360,000
$2,200	$26,400	$132,000	$264,000	$396,000
$2,400	$28,800	$144,000	$288,000	$432,000
$2,600	$31,200	$156,000	$312,000	$468,000
$2,800	$33,600	$168,000	$336,000	$504,000
$3,000	$36,000	$180,000	$360,000	$540,000
$3,500	$42,000	$210,000	$420,000	$630,000

Caveats of Homeownership

You can't deny the wealth-building power of homeownership; however, there are significant caveats that, when ignored, negate all the positive benefits of buying a home. The first is buying too much house and ending up house poor. The second is not fully understanding the costs associated with homeownership. The third is making only minimum payments on the mortgage.

Being House Poor

"House poor" is defined as a situation where a person spends a large portion of their income on homeownership, including mortgage payments, property taxes, maintenance, and utilities. After paying their mortgage and bills, people who are house poor tend to be behind on other payments, such as their car note or insurance, and have little to no disposable income.

There are two ways to become house poor: buying too much house or staying in an expensive housing situation after your income has plummeted. Regardless of how you end up in the situation, being house poor can have significant financial ramifications. People who are house poor have to deal with creeping credit card debt and the stress of continually digging into their emergency savings fund to cover day-to-day expenses, and they're usually too cash strapped to make contributions to their retirement savings.

When you begin house shopping, you will be pre-approved by lenders for a home loan up to a certain amount. For example, you may be pre-approved for up to $500,000. The problem many make is that they'll start looking at homes in the $450,000 to $500,000 range with a pre-approval of up to $500,000. Remember, one of the keys to financial wealth is living beneath your means. With a pre-approval of $500,000, you should be looking at homes in the $200,000 to $250,000 range. A home in this range is not going to be a monthly financial burden. You will be able to make these payments easily and can even throw in a few extra payments each year to get the house paid off as soon as possible.

Not Understanding All the Costs

Another way some end up house poor is by not fully understanding all the costs associated with homeownership. Depending on the area you live in, it may be cheaper to buy a home than rent; however, it's essential to realize a critical financial difference between renting and owning most overlook: Owning a home requires maintenance and upkeep. Home maintenance can be as trivial as replacing a broken window to getting your garage door repaired, or it can be as complicated as having to get a new AC system or roof.

Not being prepared for these expenses can do a number on your emergency savings fund and can even cause you to turn to your credit cards to get them taken care of. For this reason, it is recommended homeowners follow the one percent rule. According to this rule, you should set aside at least one percent of your home's value every year for maintenance. For a $250,000 house, this would come out to $2,500 per year or $209 per month.

Making Only Minimum Payments on the Mortgage

The reality is most people are not able to purchase a home in cash. For the majority of people, the purchase of a home will be facilitated through a home loan. Unfortunately, home loans involve interest.

Let's say you purchase a $175,000 home and contribute $25,000 toward the down payment. This would result in you obtaining a home loan for the remaining $150,000. If you opt for a thirty-year mortgage, you will own the home free and clear after thirty years but at the cost of a little over $260,000 in mortgage payments, assuming a 4.375% interest rate.

How does one prevent or minimize this? By making more than the minimum payments on your home loan. After you've made the monthly mortgage payment, make an extra payment of a few hundred dollars directly toward the principal of your loan. This strategy will shave years off your home loan repayment and decrease the amount of interest you pay throughout the life of the loan.

If you were to get a $150,000 home loan with a 4.375% interest rate and begin to immediately make extra monthly payments of $200 toward the principal balance, you would reduce your interest payments by over $45,000 while shaving a little over ten years off of your estimated payoff date. Instead of owning the home in thirty years, you would own it in a little over twenty.

If you were to make a higher additional monthly payment, such as $300, toward the principal balance, you're looking at even bigger savings. Your interest payments would be reduced by over $57,000, and you'd shave a little over thirteen years off of your home loan repayment.

Final Thoughts on Renting vs. Buying

At the end of the day, it's undeniable that homeownership is a catalyst for wealth. However, buying a home will be one of the most significant financial decisions you make, so be sure to consider the following:

- **Can you pay more than the minimum mortgage payments?** If you make only the minimum mortgage payments on your home loan, you will accrue a ton of interest. This is going to heavily negate the wealth-building aspects of homeownership. If you cannot make more than the minimum monthly payments on your mortgage, consider holding off on buying a home until you have more cash flow.

- **Have you been saving for a down payment?** To show lenders you are personally invested in the home you are looking to purchase, you will need to make a down payment. Down payment amounts vary, ranging all the way from 3% to 20%. Depending on the price point of the house you are looking to purchase, this can be a substantial amount of money.
- **What is your debt-to-income ratio?** Before purchasing a home, you want to pay off as much consumer debt, such as credit cards and personal loans, as you can. It doesn't make sense to add a mortgage payment to your plate if you're already struggling with your debt payments.
- **If you were to purchase a home, how long do you foresee yourself occupying it?** If you see yourself occupying the home for less than five years, it's better to rent. Five years is the average amount of time it takes to begin building equity and appreciation in your home.
- **What does your credit score look like?** A credit score of 580 is regarded as the minimum score needed for home loan eligibility. With this credit score, you qualify for a Federal Housing Administration-backed loan (also known as an FHA loan), which requires a 3.5% down payment. For a conventional loan, you would need, at minimum, a 620 credit score. Besides having access to more loan options, having a high credit score means you'll get approved at a lower interest rate.

- **Do you have an emergency savings fund?** An emergency savings fund will keep you afloat if you lose your job or face an unforeseeable emergency. You should not purchase a home until you have at minimum six months' worth of living expenses saved.
- **Can you afford to maintain the property?** We tend to focus on the monthly mortgage and down payment costs when discussing the financial aspects of home ownership, but as stated earlier in this chapter, there is another cost associated with owning a home: maintenance. As a homeowner, you will be responsible for taking care of your home and property, and that costs money.
- **Do you have the time to maintain and upkeep the property?** In addition to money, the maintenance of a home requires time. A new construction home will require less maintenance than an older home or a fixer-upper, but you'll still need to be willing and able to work on your home, regardless of its condition. Home maintenance can be as simple as changing the AC filter, or it could be something more labor intensive, such as mowing the lawn. If you don't have time to maintain your home, you'll need to have the money to pay someone else to maintain it for you. If you don't have the time or money, you should reconsider homeownership.

Whether you buy or rent depends on your wealth timeline, wealth goals, and financial situation, as well as the economics of your local area. If you plan on staying put for at least five years and making more than the minimum monthly mortgage payments on your home loan, buying a home can be a strategic addition to your wealth-building strategy. You'll have more privacy than you did as a renter, your housing costs won't fluctuate, and you'll be more prideful of your place of residence because it's all yours.

Let's not forget the most prominent benefit: A home is a sound and strategic investment you will eventually build equity in and be able to sell or pass on to the generation that comes after you. But, for some, renting is a better alternative. Sure, you miss out on the wealth-building facets of homeownership, but for those who live in a market where it is more expensive to own than rent or those who don't plan on living in the same area for the next five years, renting is a short-term commitment that comes with no down payment and little to no maintenance.

If You Decide Homeownership Is for You

Research Different Types of Financing Options

When it comes to homeownership, deciding which type of loan is right for you is just as important as picking the physical characteristics of the home you buy. There are a slew of home loans on the market with various eligibility guidelines, such as the down payment amount and the minimum credit score allowed. To be a knowledgeable buyer, you should conduct your own initial research to get educated on the loan options available. To get you started, I've compiled a list of the most commonly used home loans:

- **FHA:** Borrowers with a 580 or higher FICO credit score may qualify for an FHA loan with just 3.5% down. Borrowers with credit scores below 580 may qualify for an FHA loan, but they're required to provide a 10% down payment. Unfortunately, FHA loans come with a catch: Borrowers must pay FHA mortgage insurance. In the event of a borrower defaulting on their loan, mortgage insurance protects the lender from a loss.

- **Conventional:** 620 is the minimum credit score needed to qualify for a conventional loan. Down payment requirements start at 3%. With conventional loans, mortgage insurance is only required if you put down less than 20%.
- **USDA:** When people think of the USDA, they think of food and nutrition services, but the USDA now offers mortgages in rural areas of the country. The minimum credit score for a USDA loan is 640. USDA home loans offer incentives, such as no down payment and low mortgage insurance fees.
- **VA:** If you're a veteran, you may qualify for a VA home loan. VA loans offer a wealth of benefits, including zero down payment, one hundred percent financing, and no mortgage insurance requirement.

Get Pre-Approved

Picture this, you decide you want to buy a home, so you start browsing around on Zillow in your spare time and even dedicate a few weekends and afternoons to open houses. You find your dream home—a modern townhome located right outside the city limits—and you're about to put in an offer, only to learn you don't even qualify for it from a financial perspective. Sadly, this situation plays out all the time for those who decide to start the home-buying process without being pre-approved for a loan.

Many people mistakenly start the home-buying process by simply looking for a home. However, if you're not pre-approved for a home loan, you don't really know what you can afford and may fall in love with homes outside of your price range, ultimately wasting your time. Starting off with a pre-approval streamlines the process of buying your dream home.

Additionally, many sellers and real estate agents will only work with homebuyers who have been pre-approved. Doing so gives them peace of mind, knowing the sale isn't going to fall through. With a pre-approval, your agent will know what price points to focus on and will be able to find properties that meet your specifications and are in line with what you can afford.

Find a Real Estate Agent

The task of finding someone to represent you in a real estate transaction can seem daunting. Thanks to the internet and social media, there's not only a real estate office on every corner, but today's buyers now have online access to unlimited agents.

Sorting through these agents can be time consuming, especially for first-time homebuyers who have little to no experience with what's involved in the home-buying process. Fortunately, finding a real estate agent is neither hopeless nor improbable if you follow these steps.

Step 1: Reach out to family, friends, and neighbors.

Start your search by reaching out to your friends, family members, and neighbors to see who they used as their real estate agent, how their home-buying process went, and if based on their home-buying experience, they'd recommend the agent they used. But don't stop there! Even if they speak highly of the agent who helped them navigate their home-buying process, you still want to compare various agents, their experience, and specialties before settling on one.

Step 2: Set up interviews to screen candidates.

To begin the vetting process, call each of your potential agents to set up an interview. If you reach out to an agent and don't get a text, email, or call back within a couple of hours, go ahead and scratch them off your list. You want an agent who will be responsive, especially if you're a first-time buyer with tons of questions. Below are a few questions to ask potential agents to begin the vetting process:

- **How do you balance multiple clients?** If the potential agent has an expansive client list, ask how they ensure every client has a seamless home-buying experience. Do they have an assistant, or are there other team members who can assist you when they're busy?
- **How long have you worked as a real estate agent?** An agent's level of experience is directly correlated to how much you can rely on them for guidance, especially if you're a first-time homebuyer.
- **Is there a price point you specialize in?** If the agent specializes in multi-million-dollar listings, finding your dream home within your $350,000 to $400,000 price range may prove to be difficult.

- **What's your preferred form of communication?** Many agents take advantage of texting to verify details and dates and send reminders. But you might be someone who prefers a phone call instead. Talk to the agent to see if they're able to adapt. If they aren't, keep looking until you find an agent who can accommodate your communication preferences.
- **What neighborhoods do you cover?** You want your agent to be knowledgeable of the area you are looking to purchase your home. If you're dead set on living in a particular area and the potential agent isn't knowledgeable about that neighborhood, find someone who is.

Having the right agent plays a vital role in your home-buying experience, so don't rely solely on these questions to make your decision. After meeting with each agent, check reviews on Zillow, Yelp, Google, and Angie's List.

Step 3: Settle on one real estate agent.

You want to narrow down all your candidates to the one agent who has the knowledge and expertise to meet your home-buying needs. What typically follows is the real estate agent having you sign a buyer's agent agreement where you agree to work solely with them for a set time frame. This time frame can vary from a few weeks to several months.

Why is the agent having you sign this agreement? Most agents only get compensated on commission. During the home-buying process, when an agent is scouring through real estate databases to find properties that fit your needs, scheduling and taking you to walkthroughs, negotiating key details, answering your emails and phone calls, and even coordinating inspections, they are working for free. This agreement gives them reassurance you won't switch to another agent once they've helped you find your dream home and are in the final stages of closing. Once you sign a buyer's agent agreement, you're legally obligated to work with that agent.

Step 4: Closely review the agreement.

Buyer's agreements spell out the rights and responsibilities of both parties and the term of the agreement. Are you terrified you'll sign the agreement and end up stuck with a lousy agent who doesn't return your calls or takes you to homes that are the exact opposite of what you're looking for and completely outside of your price range? Don't be. Most of these agreements give you the right to fire the agent if they do not meet your needs. If this clause isn't in the agreement, ask the agent to include it. While buyer's agreements are necessary for an agent to work with you, they're negotiable.

Conclusion

Homeownership may seem like a distant reality to you, especially if your head is filled with limiting "I can't" thoughts. The good news is these limiting thoughts can be dissipated through education. Many people don't understand how homeownership builds wealth, nor do they have the faintest idea of how home buying works, which breeds fear.

Homeownership builds wealth by changing your financial habits for the better, acting as a vehicle for forced savings, increasing your net worth, shielding you from rent fluctuations, and allowing you to build equity that can be leveraged or passed on to the next generation of your family.

Buying a home will be one of the most significant financial decisions you make, so there's a lot you should consider, including your financial situation, the length of time you plan to stay in the home, and your ability to maintain the property, among many other things. In some circumstances, it may make sense for you to buy, while it makes sense to rent in other circumstances. It all depends on your wealth timeline, wealth goals, and financial situation, as well as the economics of your local area.

Activity

Many fear purchasing a home because they aren't fully educated on the home-buying process. For this chapter's activity, your task is to find and attend a first-time homebuyer course being held in your area. The goal of this activity is to chip away at your home-buying fears through education. A first-time homebuyer course teaches you everything you need to know about purchasing a home. Attending this course will educate you on strategies and tips to save money during the home-buying process and ways to avoid expensive mistakes. Specific topics typically discussed in the course are as follows:

- The pros and cons of homeownership
- Steps involved in the buying process
- Figuring out what you can truly afford

- Improving your credit to optimize your home loan package
- Documentation needed to secure a home loan
- Overview of the closing process
- What to look for when house hunting

To find a course being held in your area, do a quick search via your favorite search engine of "first-time homebuyer courses + the city you live in." For example, if you live in Atlanta, you would search for "first-time homebuyer courses Atlanta." Although you can, at times, find a course free of charge, most of the time, there is a cost associated with enrolling in one. In general, expect to pay between twenty-five dollars and $125, which is a drop in the bucket compared to the financial benefits of this course.

Conclusion

Congratulations! You've made it to the end of the book. It's now time to take the concepts and information you've learned and begin your wealth journey. I know you are frightened, overwhelmed, and maybe even reluctant to start because of the mistakes you made and roadblocks you encountered the last time you tried to conquer your personal finances, but this time, it's going to be different.

This time, I want you to start by setting small goals, absolutely crushing them, then working your way up to the big ones. Your wealth journey might start with saving $500, putting one of your bills on autopay, or maybe calling one of your debt collectors to set up a payment plan. You don't need to take enormous, terrifying, and daunting steps; you just need to take steps in the right direction, no matter how small.

This time, I want to make sure you don't go on this journey alone. Find a support system to keep you motivated and hold you accountable to your financial goals. Enroll in personal finance classes being held at your local community center or church. Join virtual and in-person groups, and make it a point to connect with those who are supportive of the changes you are looking to make in your life and are on a similar path.

Utilize me as a resource. Check out www.rosembellefleur.com to stay in touch and access additional personal finance books, courses, tips, advice, and resources, such as my free monthly personal finance newsletter and free monthly budget tracker.

As you progress on your wealth journey, send me your success stories so I can share them with others. Good luck, and remember, you got this!

Notes

1 "Self-Talk." *Psychology Today*, Sussex Publishers, www.psychologytoday.com/us/basics/self-talk.

2 Scott, MS, Elizabeth. "The Toxic Effects of Negative Self-Talk." Verywell Mind, 25 Feb. 2020, www.verywellmind.com/negative-self-talk-and-how-it-affects-us-4161304.

3 Schneider, Tobias Van. "If You Want It, You Might Get It. The Reticular Activating System Explained." Medium, 22 June 2017, medium.com/desk-of-van-schneider/if-you-want-it-you-might-get-it-the-reticular-activating-system-explained-761b6ac14e53.

4 Klontz, Bradley, et al. "Money Beliefs and Financial Behaviors: Development of the Klontz Money Script Inventory." *Journal of Financial Therapy*, vol. 2, no. 1, 2011, doi:10.4148/jft.v2i1.451.

5 Cazzin, Julie. "Seven Deadly Money Disorders: Underspending." *MoneySense*, 5 July 2011, www.moneysense.ca/magazine-archive/seven-deadly-money-disorders-underspending/.

6 Clarkberg, Jasper, and Michelle Kambara. "Removal of Public Records Has Little Effect on Consumers' Credit Scores." Consumer Financial Protection Bureau, 22 Feb. 2018, www.consumerfinance.gov/about-us/blog/removal-public-records-has-little-effect-consumers-credit-scores/.

7 "7 Things to Know About Fraud Alerts." 7 Things to Know About Fraud Alerts | Equifax®, www.equifax.com/personal/education/identity-theft/7-things-to-know-about-fraud-alerts/.

8 "Place a Fraud Alert." Consumer Information, FEDERAL TRADE COMMISSION, 25 Sept. 2018, www.consumer.ftc.gov/articles/0275-place-fraud-alert.

9 Elkins, Kathleen. "A Brief History of the 401(k), Which Changed How Americans Retire." CNBC, CNBC, 5 Jan. 2017, www.cnbc.com/2017/01/04/a-brief-history-of-the-401k-which-changed-how-americans-retire.html.

10 Stobierski, Tim. "401(k) Basics: When It Was Invented and How It Works." Northwestern Mutual, Northwestern Mutual, 30 Mar. 2018, www.northwesternmutual.com/life-and-money/your-401k-when-it-was-invented-and-why/.

11 History.com Editors. "Social Security Act." History.com, 26 Jan. 2018, www.history.com/topics/great-depression/social-security-act.

12 Understanding the Benefits, Social Security Administration, 2020.

13 THE 2020 ANNUAL REPORT OF THE BOARD OF TRUSTEES OF THE FEDERAL OLD-AGE AND SURVIVORS INSURANCE AND FEDERAL DISABILITY INSURANCE TRUST FUNDS, vol. 80, 2020, pp. 1–5

About the Author

Rose M. Bellefleur is a Certified Financial Education Instructor (CFEI), businesswoman, author, money coach, and motivational speaker who speaks nationally and internationally on financial literacy, financial independence, and wealth.

Rose's financial independence journey began in her early twenties. After graduating from undergrad, she found herself dealing with the repercussions of the bad financial behaviors she had allowed to fester for many years. Her money mismanagement had her dealing with very little personal savings, maxed-out credit cards, and growing debt. She decided to turn things around by setting a small goal of saving $1,000 in three months. After reaching this goal, she set another financial goal, this time to save $3,000 in six months. When she reached this goal, she set another goal of saving $12,000 in a year. The goals kept increasing in frequency and amount until she was able to save a whole year's worth of living expenses.

Impressed by her success, Rose turned her sights toward her consumer debt. She began paying off her credit card loans, medical bills, and even her car loan. Fast forward to the present, where Rose has transitioned from conquering debt to building her financial legacy by contributing aggressively to her 401(k), investing in dividend stocks, creating passive income streams, and strategically purchasing assets to increase her net worth.

Rose believes wealth is a journey, and most who suffer from financial woes lack financial education. With her debut financial self-help book *Straight to the Money: The Definitive Guide to Changing Your Mindset, Outlook, and Behaviors to Attract Wealth,* she seeks to provide an accessible entrance to this education by sharing the approaches that led her from drowning in debt to a comfortable financial foundation and a greater understanding of how wealth is built.

Now, Rose works to help others build wealth by changing their mindset toward and relationship with money. Additionally, she provides financial literacy coaching to help others take control of their future and give them the confidence to tackle wealth goals, like paying off debt, growing their savings, increasing their credit scores, and investing.

Rose has earned a master of professional studies in technology management from Georgetown University, a graduate certificate in marketing strategy from Cornell University, and a bachelor of business administration in marketing from Georgia State University.

Questions for Discussion

1. Have you ever suffered from negative self-talk? If so, describe a time when your negative self-talk held you back from reaching a goal.
2. Define compound interest as if you were talking to a five-year-old. How does it create wealth? In what instances does it prevent you from building wealth?
3. What money script best aligns with your financial thoughts, perspectives, and behaviors?
4. In the city you live in, is it cheaper to own or rent a home? If it is cheaper to own, how much do you pay for rent currently, and what would your monthly mortgage payments look like if you owned a home?
5. How does homeownership build wealth? In what instances would it not build wealth?
6. What percentage of your monthly income comes from your day job? Outside of this day job, do you have any other sources of income?

7. Imagine a scenario where there is no such thing as failure and you have $10,000 to put toward an entrepreneurship venture. What business idea would you bring to life?
8. Do you currently live at, above, or below your means?
9. On a monthly basis, what non-essential expense accounts for the bulk of your spending?
10. What financial plans have you put in place to fund your retirement?
11. What are the two highest debts you owe? What is the interest rate associated with each of these debts?
12. Describe dividend income as if you were talking to a five-year-old.
13. What would your account balance be in forty years if you deposited $15,000 into an account compounded annually at a 5% interest rate?
14. What is the current balance of your 401(k)? What is the projected balance if you were to retire at the age of sixty-five?
15. How much money is typically left in your bank account after paying all of your monthly bills?

Thank you for reading *Straight to the Money*
If you enjoyed this book or found it useful, please
help spread the word with an online review.

KEEP UP WITH
ROSE M. BELLEFLEUR

Website: www.rosembellefleur.com
Facebook: Rose M. Bellefleur
Instagram: @rosembellefleur

Made in the USA
Monee, IL
08 November 2026

67378303R10111